THE LITTLE GUIDES

DINOSAURS

THE LITTLE GUIDES

DINOSAURS

CONSULTANT EDITOR
Dr. Paul Willis

FOG CITY PRESS

Published by Fog City Press
814 Montgomery Street
San Francisco, CA 94133 USA

FOG CITY PRESS
Chief Executive Officer: John Owen
President: Terry Newell
Publisher: Lynn Humphries
Managing Editor: Janine Flew
Design Manager: Helen Perks
Editorial Coordinator: Kiren Thandi
Production Manager: Caroline Webber
Production Coordinator: James Blackman
Sales Manager: Emily Jahn
Vice President International Sales: Stuart Laurence

LIMELIGHT PRESS PTY LTD
Project Manager and Editor: Helen Bateman
Consultant Editor: Dr. Paul Willis
Designer: Avril Makula

A catalog record for this book is available from
the Library of Congress, Washington. DC.

ISBN 1 877019 53 4

Color reproduction by Colourscan Co Pte Ltd
Printed by LeeFung-Asco Printers
Printed in China

A Weldon Owen Production

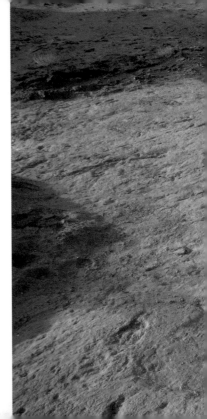

CONTENTS

PART THREE
DINOSAUR GUIDE

USING THE DINOSAUR GUIDE 158

PART ONE

THE WORLD OF THE DINOSAURS

UNDERSTANDING THE PAST

Only quite recently has science resolved many of the mysteries of the world the dinosaurs inhabited. Answers to questions about the distant past can be found in ancient rocks and the fossils they contain. Over the past couple of centuries, the sciences of paleontology and geology have painted for us an increasingly clear and diverse picture about past eras and the life forms that existed in them—a picture that was previously the realm of mere speculation. Though this picture is far from complete, missing pieces are constantly being found. We now realize that dinosaurs were an extremely successful group of animals that occupied all the lands of the world for 160 million years.

READING THE ROCKS

Rocks that have built up in layers over millions of years have provided the vital clues to the age of the Earth and the life forms that have inhabited it at different times in its history. Over the past 250 years, geologists have built up a picture of the Earth's past by examining how rocks form and how they are placed in relation to each other.

Layers of rock For many years, geologists have known that the rocks of the Earth's surface are layered one on top of the other, like a stack of books. It follows, then, that the rocks situated at the bottom of the pile must have been laid down before those rocks that are closer to the top. By using this principle, geologists are able to work out the relative ages of rocks by observing how the different types of rocks are arranged with respect to each other.

The stratigraphic column
By systematically mapping all the world's known rocks and working out their relative positions, geologists have assembled what we call the stratigraphic column. This is a register, or diagram, of the relative ages of different types of rocks.

Eras, periods and epochs The stratigraphic column spans almost the complete 4,600-million-year history of the Earth. This is a huge collection of information, so in order to make it easier to understand, geologists have divided it up into a number of sections that we call the geological eras, periods and epochs.

Dinosaur times The Mesozoic era, during which the dinosaurs lived, lasted for 180 million years, from 245 to 65 million years ago. It is divided into three periods. The earliest (the Triassic period, which ended 208 million years ago) is a section of the stratigraphic column that lies underneath a younger section, the Jurassic period, which ended 145 million years ago. On top of the Jurassic are the rocks of the Cretaceous, the longest and most recent of the three periods of the Mesozoic era. The Cretaceous lasted for 80 million years, from 145 to 65 million years ago. The periods of the Mesozoic and the

DIFFERENT STRATA

Reddish sandstones, shales, mudstones and siltstones are among the many layers that can be distinguished in the cliffs of Arizona's Grand Canyon.

IN THE FIELD

Field work takes geologists to many places—the tops of mountains, into underground caverns and even to the seabed to look at ancient sediments.

READING THE ROCKS continued

eras that came before and after it are further divided into smaller segments, which are known as epochs and stages.

Dating rocks Paleontologists calculate times by looking at the degree of decay that is displayed by particular elements found in certain types of rocks. The longer the rock has been in existence, the greater the decay that will have taken place. These techniques provide "absolute" time or age, which scientists then measure in millions of years. When combined with information from the stratigraphic column, they allow us to allocate dates to other rock units. It comes as no surprise that the dates given by absolute dating techniques agree with the order of dates given to us from the stratigraphic column.

DEEP IN THE PAST
By studying the rocks and other clues in the walls of the Grand Canyon in Arizona, geologists can paint a picture of the canyon's history, which dates back more than 2,000 million years.

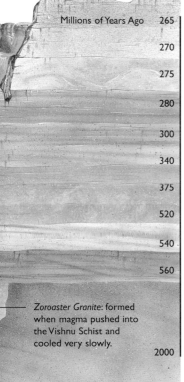

Millions of Years Ago   265

Kaibab Limestone: contains the remains of sea creatures.

270

Toroweap Sandstone: formed from sand deposited by a sea.

275

Coconino Sandstone: the remains of a vast desert.

280

Hermit Shale: formed from silt deposited by a river system.

300

Supai Group: sandstone ledges and slopes formed from mud and sand deposited by rivers and oceans.

340

Redwall Limestone: contains the remains of later marine creatures.

375

Temple Butte Limestone: formed as more creatures lived and died in the warm sea.

520

Muav Limestone: formed from the remains of early sea creatures.

540

Bright Angel Shale: formed from muds and silts deposited in the sea as it flooded the land.

560

Tapeats Sandstone: the remains of a beach that formed as a sea moved in over the old eroded mountains.

Zoroaster Granite: formed when magma pushed into the Vishnu Schist and cooled very slowly.

2000

Vishnu Schist: a metamorphic rock that formed part of a huge mountain range. The range was created two billion years ago when two continents collided.

FOSSILS

Rocks often contain traces of ancient life. These are called fossils. Fossils are the vital clues on which the laborious but fascinating detective work of paleontology is based. They can be footprints, bones, impressions or other signs of prehistoric plants or animals. Fossils form when living things walk on or die in swamp, lake, river or ocean sediments.

The beginnings When these sediments harden into rock, they may retain the impression of the original life form. Sometimes, minerals replace parts of the dead animals or plants and gradually turn them into rock.

Ancient and newer fossils
The world has been in existence for 4,600 million years, and fossils have been found dating back 3,800 million years, but evidence for complex life does not appear until around 600 million years ago. Fossils that date back farther than this are relatively scarce. However, a more abundant supply of more recent fossils has allowed scientists to plot the course of evolution and the development of life. As various types of animals and plant forms have come into existence and become extinct, many of them have left their fossils behind in the rocks within the stratigraphic column, serving as a record for paleontologists.

TREE FOSSIL
This fossilized tree, from the Jurassic period, forms part of a fossil forest at Lulworth Cove, in Dorset, UK. These fossils have been dated to between 162 and 135 million years ago.

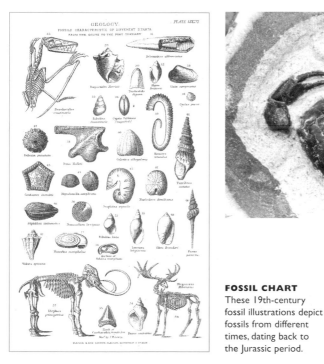

JURASSIC CRAB FOSSIL
This fossilized crab was found in
Jurassic deposits in Australia. Shelly
fossils like these are more abundant
and widespread than fossils of animals
such as dinosaurs.

FOSSIL CHART
These 19th-century
fossil illustrations depict
fossils from different
times, dating back to
the Jurassic period.

FOSSILS: HOW FOSSILS FORM

FIRST STAGE OF FOSSILIZATION
A *Camptosaurus*, a late Jurassic dinosaur, has died of disease or old age. If scavengers do not destroy the bones, it will be covered with silt and gradually fossilized.

Fossil candidates Fossils are records, written in stone or rock, of life through the ages. Anything that was once alive can leave fossil traces, but some organisms are better candidates for fossilization than others. Usually, only the hard parts of a plant or animal end up as fossils. Muscles, skin and internal organs are rarely preserved. The shells of animals such as clams and snails and the bones of vertebrates are much more likely to be preserved than are the bodies of soft animals, such as worms and jellyfish. Indeed, the fossil record of these creatures is almost nonexistent. In certain instances, eggs, footprints and dung can also fossilize.

Fossil processes There are a number of ways that fossils can form. Most fossils, however, result from the burial of an organism's remains in the sediments of a river, lake or sea. Once the soft tissues have rotted away, the bones or shell become encased in the surrounding mud and silts. As time passes, these sediments harden into rocks, and the bones or shell that are trapped within create an impression of their living form. Sometimes, the actual remains are completely replaced, cell by cell, with minerals that wash through the enveloping rock—a process that is called "petrification." In other cases, the bone dissolves, leaving behind a hole—a natural mold in the rock that can later fill with minerals. Other fossils are created in less usual ways. Insects and small animals, for example, can become trapped in tree sap that hardens and seals in a copy of the animal. Sometimes, the mineral silica can fill the impressions in the rock left behind by an animal, resulting in a fossil shell or skeleton.

HOW FOSSILS FORM continued

Shells and plants By far the greatest number of fossils are the remains of shelled creatures that lived in shallow seas. Coral, clams, snails and a host of other invertebrate animals make up the bulk of the world's fossil collection. More rarely, plants can become fossilized. Coal, for example, is the fossil remains of whole forests. Only rarely, though, do any traces of plant structure survive. Plant structures are destroyed as the coal is compressed to less than one-hundredth the thickness of the once-living plants that comprise it.

Land animals The remains of animals that once lived on land are fossilized even more rarely than those of plants. In order to be candidates for fossilization, these animals need to have died close to or in a watercourse that floods and buries its prize in muds and silts. The fact that, at least as far as we know, all dinosaurs lived on land explains the scarcity of their fossil remains and makes it all the more likely that we will never know just how diverse they really were.

Footprints and nests Animals that walked or ran across tidal flats or floodplains have left a record of their passing as fossilized footprints. Sometimes, the trackways of whole herds have been preserved. In some cases, complete rookeries of dinosaur nests have been inundated and are now preserved as fossils.

FOOTPRINTS
The fine-grained sandstone of the Winton Formation, in Queensland, Australia, has preserved thousands of dinosaur footprints.

1. SAFE FROM SCAVENGERS
Beneath the surface of a lake, a dead dinosaur's remains are safe from large scavengers. Its flesh rots away or is eaten by fish and the skeleton remains intact.

2. COVERING UP
Over a long period of time, layers of sand or silt accumulate over the dinosaur's bones. This sets them in place and prevents them from being washed away.

3. FOSSILIZING
The dinosaur's bones are increasingly trapped and flattened by growing layers of sediment. Gradually, these bones are replaced by minerals that are harder than the rocks that surround them.

4. COMING TO LIGHT
Millions of years later, seismic disturbances in the Earth's crust bring the dinosaur's fossilized skeleton close to the surface, where it is gradually exposed by the weather and erosion.

FOSSILS: DATING FOSSILS

FISH FOSSIL
This fish fossil has been dated to the Eocene period, between 35 million and 23 million years ago.

Dating techniques There are several methods of directly dating some types of rock. One, known as radiometric dating, measures the degree of decay of various isotopes (forms of a chemical element) contained in particular minerals in the rock. Another, paleomagnetic dating, measures the ancient magnetism of the rock. Yet another, fission-track dating, examines the effects of uranium breakdown in zircon crystals.

Radiometric dating One of the most widely used radiometric dating techniques measures the rate of decay of the isotope potassium 40 to form the gas argon 40. A small proportion of naturally occurring potassium includes potassium 40, which decays at a steady, and known, rate to produce argon 40. When a rock is molten, any accumulated argon gas can escape. Once the rock solidifies, the argon gas starts to build up again inside it. The longer the time since the rock solidified, the greater the amount of argon gas that accumulates. By measuring the amount of argon 40 gas relative to the amount of potassium 40 in a rock, we get an accurate measure of how long it is since the rock solidified.

Paleomagnetic dating The Earth's magnetic poles sometimes flip over. A record of these flips is held within once-molten rocks such as basalt. Magnetic reversal events vary in length, but their history is preserved on the ocean floors. Study of the magnetic orientation of basalts on land can match them to the history from the sea floor, and the age of the basalt and its surrounding rocks can be determined.

Fission-track dating Uranium occurs naturally in zircon. An unstable isotope of uranium, U238, undergoes nuclear fission, which leaves small scratches on zircon crystals. Counting these fission scratches allows scientists to determine the age of a crystal.

FOSSILS IN ROCKS

By dating the layers of rocks that are found at different levels, scientists can determine the age of the fossils found in them.

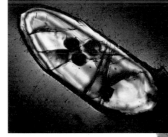

ZIRCON CRYSTAL

By using fission-track dating, scientists have been able to calculate that this zircon crystal found in Western Australia is 4,100 million years old.

FOSSILS: TYPES OF DINOSAUR FOSSILS

Study of fossils Fossils are the remains of once-living organisms. It is the job of the paleontologist to reconstruct the life of extinct animals based on the fossils they have left behind. Dinosaur fossils are among the most intensively studied fossils of all. Everything we know, or can conjecture, about dinosaurs and how they lived is based on what fossil remains can reveal.

Bones and skeletons The most common dinosaur fossils are individual bones and other fragments, such as teeth, and, more rarely, complete skeletons. From these finds, paleontologists are able to construct theories and draw conclusions about the evolution of dinosaurs—what different species were like in life, and how they were related to each other and to other creatures that lived at the same time. Although they are relatively rare, skeletons give much more information than separate bones. Complete skeletons have been found of only very few dinosaurs. However, most of the major groups of dinosaurs include at least one member for

HORNED SKULL
The first complete skull of the late Cretaceous horned dinosaur *Triceratops* was found in Wyoming in 1889.

ANCIENT BONES
These hadrosaur bones, dating back to the late Cretaceous, are in the Dinosaur Provincial Park in Alberta, Canada.

which a skeleton is known. Skeletons help us to reconstruct the missing pieces of other dinosaurs that are known only from fragmentary remains, or even single bones.

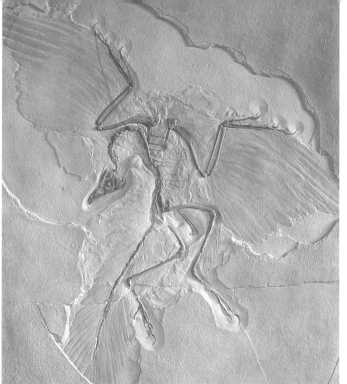

FULL SKELETON

Seven full skeletons of *Archaeopteryx* have been found. Five of them show impressions of the delicate feathers that this dinosaur had in life.

BABY FOSSILS

A fossilized embryo of *Oviraptor* (left) and skull fragments of a baby dromaeosaur (right) are in the collection of New York's American Museum of Natural History.

TYPES OF DINOSAUR FOSSILS continued

Rarer fossils Non-bone fossils, such as eggs, dung, footprints and trackways, also provide valuable insights into how dinosaurs lived. The rarest of dinosaur fossils preserve such soft tissue as skin, feathers, muscle or, very rarely, internal organs. These delicate structures are easily destroyed and exceptional circumstances are required for them to fossilize. Feathers are best known from some of the specimens of *Archaeopteryx*, although recent finds in China have also revealed dinosaurs with feathers and featherlike structures attached. Dung fossils, or coprolites, can show what dinosaurs ate and can give an idea of some anatomical structures. However, it is difficult to link coprolites to the dinosaurs that produced them. Fossil finds of eggs and embryos have been known for more than 100 years, but have only been studied in detail in recent years. They have provided a wealth of information about dinosaur development, reproduction and behavior.

EARLY EGG FIND
This nest, which contained eggs of *Oviraptor* (many of which were still intact), was discovered in 1922 during one of several American expeditions to Mongolia during the 1920s.

TRACKWAYS

The famous American paleontologist Barnum Brown is seen here marking out a group of fossilized footprints of theropod dinosaurs.

FEATHERS

Sinornithosaurus, an early Cretaceous dinosaur, was discovered in China in 1999. It showed evidence of featherlike structures on the body.

FOSSILS: INTERPRETING FOSSILS

CELL STRUCTURE
The cell structure of a fossilized Jurassic dinosaur bone can be seen in this section of a bone from the Morrison Formation in Colorado, USA.

An emerging picture Bones and other fossil remains paint a cumulative picture of the evolutionary changes that dinosaurs experienced over time. Coupled with evidence of age, gained from the radiometric dating of rocks, changes of bone structure can be used to reconstruct dinosaurs'

evolutionary history. Bones and skeletons are also our starting point in rebuilding the size and appearance of an extinct creature. They can also provide important clues about the soft parts of a dinosaur that have not fossilized. The paleontologist must be conscious that the features of these bones are clues to the ways in which they served a living animal. For example, bones from the "hands" of a dinosaur that walked on all fours will be more robust than the same bones of a relative that walked with its hands free. Again, sharp claws are for slashing or holding, blunt claws are for walking on. Meat-eaters require sharp teeth for ripping flesh; plant-eaters need grinding teeth to pulp their food. Muscles attach to bones and leave scars. Careful study of the size and position of these scars can reveal the way in which the animal moved a limb and how strong it was. Dinosaurs' brains were encased in bone and, even though the brain is never fossilized, the space in which it was housed can give a good idea of what the living brain was like.

Diseases and injuries Diseases and injuries suffered by an animal can be reflected in bone fossils. Cancers, arthritis, gout and other disorders have been identified in dinosaurs from bone fossils. Injuries detected include broken bones and gouges from fighting. Much can also be learned from the arrangement of bones where they are discovered. An intact skeleton reveals a quick burial after death, whereas a scattered collection of bones may indicate that the carcass was scavenged. Isolated bones may have been carried off by a predator or washed away in a flood.

SAUROPOD FOOTPRINTS
Trackways provide clues about how dinosaurs moved. These herbivores walked on all fours. The large prints are from the back feet.

SMALL THEROPOD FOOTPRINTS
These swift-moving small carnivores left tracks that are delicate and birdlike. They moved on their hindlimbs.

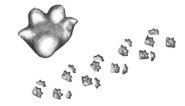

CERATOPSIAN FOOTPRINTS
These horned plant-eaters walked on all four legs. Their front feet made the smaller prints.

LARGE THEROPOD FOOTPRINTS
Like the smaller theropods, these large carnivores moved on their hindlimbs. Their back feet each had three toes.

DISCOVERING DINOSAURS

We will never know who discovered the first dinosaur fossil, or even when or where it was found. The first known description of a dinosaur bone was published by Robert Plot in England in 1677. It was almost certainly the base of a theropod femur, possibly that of *Megalosaurus*. Plot described it merely as an "enigmatic thighbone."

Dinosaurs recognized A major breakthrough in the understanding of dinosaur fossils occurred about 1818, when the English naturalist Dean William Buckland began a systematic survey of animal fossils from all over England. In 1822, Buckland identified some bones from Oxfordshire as belonging to a beast that he named *Megalosaurus* (meaning "giant lizard"). This represented a pioneering move toward the recognition of dinosaurs as extinct reptiles.

Mantell In 1825 an English dentist, Gideon Mantell, reported on some fossils that were found in Sussex. These finds included a conical bone and some teeth that closely resembled those of a living iguana. Mantell named the find *Iguanodon*, and concluded that this now extinct animal was a giant variant of the living form. At the time both *Megalosaurus* and *Iguanodon* were wrongly assumed to be large quadrupeds, and early reconstructions reflected this.

NAMER OF REPTILES
Edward Drinker Cope of the Academy of Natural Sciences in Philadelphia probably named more reptiles, living and extinct, than any other researcher.

ALBERTA DISCOVERY
Charles H. Sternberg led his family of three sons in a fossil-hunting business. In 1917, in Alberta, Canada, he found fossil remains of *Albertosaurus libratus*.

CHINA SEARCHERS
Roy Chapman Andrews (left) and Walter Granger were American paleontologists who made important dinosaur discoveries in China and Mongolia in the 1920s.

DISCOVERING DINOSAURS continued

BRAIN EXPERT

Canadian Dale Russell now works in the United States. He specializes in theropod dinosaurs, and has named several new species. Much of his earlier work involved studies of dinosaur brains and endocasts.

Owen New dinosaurs continued to be discovered in Britain and other places, but it was not until the 1840s that the great English anatomist and paleontologist Sir Richard Owen recognized that all these animals shared certain distinctive features and so belonged together as a group. He gave them the class name "Dinosauria."

A first golden age Between 1870 and 1890, a series of new dinosaur finds in the American West made by expeditions led by Othniel Charles Marsh and Edward Drinker Cope, is the beginning of the first golden age of dinosaur paleontology. Friends at first, Cope and Marsh soon became bitter rivals. This rivalry,

however, led to the discovery of many now familiar dinosaurs, including *Apatosaurus*, *Diplodocus*, *Allosaurus* and *Triceratops*. Other researchers, such as Barnum Brown, Henry Fairfield Osborn and Charles H. Sternberg, carried on the work that Cope and Marsh began in North America. Osborn and Brown are celebrated especially for their discovery, in 1905 in Montana, of *Tyrannosaurus rex*. Sternberg, who worked mainly in Alberta, Canada, brought to light, among many others, *Albertosaurus*, *Edmontonia* and *Lambeosaurus*.

WYOMING FIND

During the 1890s, Barnum Brown (right) and Henry Fairfield Osborn developed a *Diplodocus* prospect at Como Bluff, in Wyoming.

RICH FINDS

Tom Rich and Patricia Vickers-Rich have made many finds in Mesozoic and Tertiary deposits in Victoria, Australia. Their most famous site is Dinosaur Cove, on the southern coast of the Australian mainland.

SIGNIFICANT FOSSILS WERE
DISCOVERED AT THIS LOCALITY,
DINOSAUR COVE, IN 1980.
FIELD PARTIES COMPOSED
PRINCIPALLY OF VOLUNTEERS
FROM MONASH UNIVERSITY,
THE MUSEUM OF VICTORIA
AND EARTHWATCH COLLECTED
DINOSAURS AND OTHER
VERTEBRATE FOSSILS FROM
THREE SITES WITHIN THIS COVE,
1984 - 1993. MAJOR SUPPORT CAME
FROM THE NATIONAL GEOGRAPHIC
SOCIETY, ATLAS COPCO, I.C.I.,
THE DEPARTMENT OF CONSERVATION
& NATURAL RESOURCES, AND
THE AUSTRALIAN RESEARCH

DISCOVERING DINOSAURS continued

Farther afield The majority of the significant late 19th-century finds were made in North America. This changed in 1907, when important new discoveries were made by a German expedition led by Dr. Werner Janensch at Tendaguru, in what is now Tanzania. These included a massive skeleton of *Brachiosaurus* that is still on display in the Berlin Museum. Later, in the 1920s, significant discoveries were made in China and Mongolia. Expeditions sent from America to Mongolia at this time yielded a wealth of dinosaur finds, including the first dinosaur eggs and remains of *Oviraptor*, *Protoceratops* and *Velociraptor*.

A new golden age The first golden age ended in the 1930s, largely because paleontologists became preoccupied with issues other than dinosaurs. However, another golden age, which is still continuing, began in the 1970s.

A worldwide activity

Dinosaur research and discovery is now a worldwide activity. While research and discovery continue apace in North America, many of the most exciting finds in recent times have been made in Liaoning, in China; in the Ischigualasto Formation, in Argentina; and in various parts of Australia. One of the most famous of modern paleontologists, Professor Dong Zhiming from China, is a prolific discoverer and namer of new Chinese dinosaurs.

NEW VIEW
In the 1970s and 1980s, scientist Robert Bakker, seen here with a *Stegosaurus* reconstruction, helped to promote a "new view" of dinosaurs as active, agile and birdlike.

TORRID WORK

Paul Sereno, of the University of Chicago, is seen here in the Moroccan Sahara, unearthing the jaw of a *Carcharodontosaurus*.

POLISH EXPEDITIONS

Zofia Kielan-Jaworowska headed three joint Polish–Mongolian expeditions to the Gobi Desert, in Mongolia, between 1963 and 1971. One of their most important discoveries was the claws and arms of *Deinocheirus*.

WORKING WITH DINOSAURS

Many kinds of people work with dinosaur fossils. They include fossil-hunters, amateur as well as professional, laboratory scientists and their assistants and a range of technicians who prepare fossils for display or for study in museums.

In the field Paleontologists usually start their search for fossils in places where fossils have already been found. The badlands of Montana and South Dakota, USA, for example, have been searched over and over again because they have proved a rich resource and because ongoing erosion is likely to reveal new specimens. At other times, searchers go to places that have not been investigated before, but where, as they have learnt from training and experience, the rocks are of the right age and type to contain dinosaur fossils. The search is a time-consuming business. Paleontologists spend long hours walking about looking for likely clues. Small bone chips are one sign. If these are scattered over a wide area, they can often be traced back to their origin, which could prove the right place to start digging. Dinosaur fossils are heavy, but fragile. Workers painstakingly dig with shovels, picks, brushes and trowels to expose the fossils. The fossils are then hardened with special chemicals and wrapped in plaster and burlap. Finally, they are loaded onto trucks to be transported to the museum.

ESSENTIAL TOOLS
A variety of tools is needed to uncover and extract fossils from rock or earth and to prepare them for transportation to the laboratory or museum.

LOCAL LABOR
Between 1909 and 1912 a German expedition excavated fossils at Tendaguru in Tanzania. Local workers did the digging and carried the fossils long distances to the nearest seaport.

WORKING WITH DINOSAURS continued

MAP WORK

Mapping the site of a fossil find is an important part of the field work. Here, a scientist employs a grid to map out the site of a fossil find in Shell, Wyoming, USA.

Museum preparation At the museum, fossils are subjected to a long process of unpacking, cleaning, conservation and identification. Once the protective packaging has been removed, technicians brush the fossils clean of dust and surface grit and then carefully remove any rock that is still attached. An array of fine chisels and saws, dental picks and drills, engraving tools and small air-powered abrasive instruments are used. Freshly exposed pieces of fossil are hardened or reinforced with glues or special plastics. Broken bones are glued together again. Paleontologists now begin a detailed study of the specimen, looking out for features that may help to identify it. If the specimen turns out to be a new type of dinosaur, it is named and fully described in scientific journals.

KEEPING RECORDS

Specially trained artists record fossil finds in detail. Their drawings, along with written descriptions, are of great importance in disseminating information to scientists around the world.

New dinosaur discoveries often attract wide media coverage.

Reconstruction It is rare for a complete skeleton to be found. Scientists, therefore, try to fill in the missing bones. To do this accurately, researchers rely on their sound knowledge of anatomy and their familiarity with many different types of dinosaurs.

Vital support Reconstructed dinosaur skeletons in museums are usually held together by strong metal frames. Long necks and tails or large heads are often supported by steel wires attached to ceilings.

Fossilized bone is usually too heavy to mount safely in a display, and fossil material that is part of an exhibit is not readily available for further study. So sometimes, expertly made fiberglass replicas, rather than the actual fossils, are what we see in museum displays.

CLASSIFYING DINOSAURS

Biologists use a method of classifying living things that reflects the relationships between them. This system of classification is known as taxonomy. It was developed by the 18th century Swedish naturalist Carl Linnaeus.

Linnaeus Carl Linnaeus assigned to all known plants and animals a two-part name, which identifies both their genus and their species. A genus is a collection of closely related species. A species is a population, or group, of individual organisms that is distinguished by the fact that they can interbreed with each other, but not with other living things. Another important innovation that Linnaeus made was to rank similar organisms according to their degree of similarity. Similar species are grouped into a genus, similar genera are grouped into families, families are grouped into orders, and so on. The higher we go in this hierarchy of groups, the less similarity there is between the individual members of the group.

EVOLUTIONIST

In 1859, Charles Darwin published *On the Origin of Species*, in which he propounded his theory of evolution. This theory claimed that all living things were related by descent.

Darwin Eighty years after Linnaeus developed his system, Charles Darwin's theory of evolution gave added sense to these classifications by suggesting that organisms are related because they share a common descent. The more recently organisms have diverged from each other, the more similar they appear.

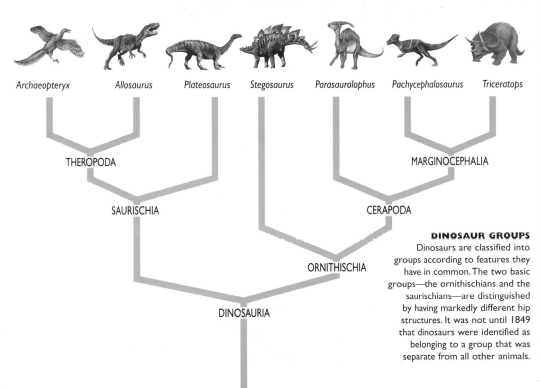

Archaeopteryx   Allosaurus   Plateosaurus   Stegosaurus   Parasaurolophus   Pachycephalosaurus   Triceratops

THEROPODA   MARGINOCEPHALIA

SAURISCHIA   CERAPODA

ORNITHISCHIA

DINOSAURIA

DINOSAUR GROUPS

Dinosaurs are classified into groups according to features they have in common. The two basic groups—the ornithischians and the saurischians—are distinguished by having markedly different hip structures. It was not until 1849 that dinosaurs were identified as belonging to a group that was separate from all other animals.

41

THE AGE OF DINOSAURS

For more than 160 million years, from when they first appeared in the late Triassic period until they became extinct at the end of the Cretaceous, the dinosaurs were the dominant land animals on Earth. We will never know for certain why dinosaurs enjoyed such a long dominance. Some argue their advanced system of locomotion and others that they were simply filling an ecological void. Although they had many features in common, the dinosaurs were a greatly diverse group that varied enormously in size, physical form, diet and lifestyle. In this section you will read about their evolution and development and about the differing eras in which they lived and died.

BEFORE THE DINOSAURS

The Earth's long history is divided into different periods, during each of which an amazing range of life forms developed and died out. The Earth began about 4,600 million years ago.

The Precambrian era In the Precambrian era, which lasted for almost 4,000 million years, single-celled algae and bacteria formed, or evolved, in the seas that covered most of the planet. In the latter part of the Precambrian era, the first animals with soft bodies and many cells made their appearance.

In the sea In the early Paleozoic era, more complex marine plants and animals, such as sponges, segmented worms and the first hard-shelled animals appeared. Later, bony fish evolved and ate the worms and jellyfish that were now abundant in the seas.

On land Amphibians, which preyed on land animals and plants, evolved from fish with lungs and strong fins. Some amphibians then evolved into reptiles that did not lay their eggs in water. Early reptiles evolved into turtles, lizards, tortoises, early mammals, birds and dinosaurs, which dominated the world for millions of years.

AMMONITES
These shelled marine carnivores of varying shapes and sizes evolved in the Cambrian period and became extinct, along with the dinosaurs and many other creatures, at the end of the Cretaceous period.

CAVALCADE OF LIFE
From the beginning of the Earth to the end of the Permian period, life evolved from single-celled algae and bacteria, through a variety of sea creatures, to early mammal-like reptiles, which were ancestors of the dinosaurs.

TRILOBITE
Trilobites were among the first hard-shelled animals. They came on the scene in the Cambrian period, more than 500 million years ago.

BEFORE THE DINOSAURS continued

Archosaurs Archosaurs are a group of animals that included the last common ancestors of living birds and living crocodilians. They first appeared early in the Mesozoic era, which followed the Paleozoic era, but it was only in the middle of the Triassic period that they began to dominate the Earth's dry-land habitats. The first archosaur would have looked like a strange cross between a crocodile and a dog. Although the ancestral archosaur remains undiscovered, we can get an idea of its probable appearance with *Euparkeria*, from the Triassic of South Africa. It measured about 2 feet (60 cm) long and was probably a predatory animal with sharp teeth and strong jaws. Dinosaurs evolved from the archosaurs near the end of the Triassic period. Earlier ancestors were crocodile-like reptiles, whose

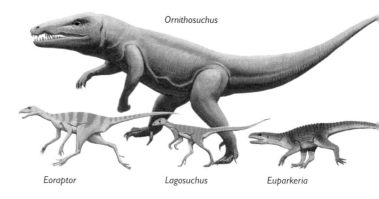

Ornithosuchus

Eoraptor   Lagosuchus   Euparkeria

legs sprawled to the sides of their bodies. *Euparkeria* had straighter legs and carried its body off the ground. Later archosaurs had legs tucked beneath their bodies and could walk on their hind legs. The predatory archosaur *Ornithosuchus* appeared in the late Triassic, and it looked a little like a dinosaur.

FEATURES IN COMMON
Throughout the Triassic period, archosaurs evolved some of the features of the later dinosaurs. The first known dinosaur, *Eoraptor*, appeared about 228 million years ago.

Millions of years ago	Era	Period		
290–245		Permian		Many species of reptiles that ate plants and meat. Trilobites disappear.
362–290		Carboniferous		The age of amphibians. Primitive reptiles appear.
408–362	Paleozoic	Devonian		The age of fishes and the first land animals with backbones.
439–408		Silurian		First land plants. Sea scorpions up to 2 m (7 ft) dominated the seas.
510–439		Ordovician		First animals with backbones, followed by jawless fish, then sharks and bony fish.
570–510		Cambrian		First sponges, segmented worms and hard-shelled animals.
2500–570	Precambrian	Proterozoic		First animals with soft bodies and many cells.
4600–2500		Archaean		First algae and single-celled bacteria appeared in the seas.

Origin of the Earth

DIMETRODON

Dimetrodon was a synapsid—a small, mammal-like reptile. It was an ancestor of the archosaurs and the dinosaurs that lived in the Permian period.

47

THE TRIASSIC PERIOD

The first dinosaurs appeared sometime during the late Triassic, roughly 228 million years ago, in an environment which would be unrecognizable to us. It was a world in which there was only one major landmass, where there were dry, red landscapes and forests without a single flower.

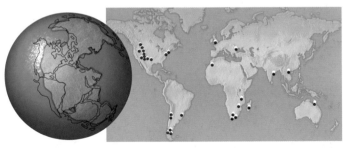

WORLD VIEW
In the Triassic, the continents formed one huge supercontinent, Pangea. At that time it was the world's only large landmass.

TRIASSIC DINOSAUR SITES
This present-day map shows those parts of the modern world in which fossils of dinosaurs from the Triassic period have been found.

Pangea the supercontinent
At various times in the past, all the Earth's landmasses have been joined. One of those periods spans the boundary between the Paleozoic and Mesozoic eras, when today's continents were joined in the single landmass of Pangea. North America, Europe and much of Asia formed the northern part of Pangea, while the southern part consisted of South America, Africa, Australia, India and Antarctica.

Changes At the beginning of the Triassic, this supercontinent extended from the South Pole to the middle of the Northern Hemisphere, and it gradually drifted northward. At the end of the Triassic, Pangea was centered on the equator. Consequently, climates changed, growing gradually warmer and drier.

INSECT PREY

Near the coast in Triassic times, forests were alive with insects, such as dragonflies, which were food for many carnivorous dinosaurs.

AGILE HUNTER

One of the earliest dinosaurs, *Coelophysis* was a fast-moving predator that used its clawed hands to grab small prey, such as the tiny *Planocephalosaurus* that is trying to escape up this tree.

THE TRIASSIC PERIOD continued

Climate change Scientists agree that global climates were seasonal during the second half of the Triassic period, with alternating warm–cool and wet–dry cycles. Worldwide climate was probably warmer and drier than it is today, with a broad arid belt in the middle of Pangea and with more humid conditions predominating toward the northern and southern ends of the supercontinent. Many late Triassic rocks represent ancient sand dunes, and they tend to be red as a result of oxidized iron. This is an indication of arid conditions, according to some paleoclimatologists. Evaporites, which are minerals that form when salty water evaporates, are common in late Triassic deposits.

Fauna When continents collide, giant mountain ranges arise. This is still happening today in the Himalayas, where India is pushing into the rest of Asia. It also occurred when Pangea formed, but by the time the dinosaurs appeared, these mountain ranges were old and weathered down. As a result, and also because climates were broadly uniform throughout Pangea, there was little to prevent

TRIASSIC VEGETATION

The Triassic landscape was mainly arid, but, especially in regions near water, there were richly vegetated pockets where plant life thrived. Needle-trees, similar to living Norfolk Island pines, and monkey-puzzle trees, some of which were very tall, grew during the Triassic. Ferns, including tree ferns, were common and diverse; and cycads, thick-leaved plants that outwardly resembled palms, were common. There were, however, no flowering plants.

animals from spreading far and wide. If you could travel through time back to Pangea in the late Triassic, you would see a range of animal life. On the land would be herds of small, usually bipedal, dinosaurs, as well as small, shrewlike early relatives of mammals and crocodiles that looked more like reptilian wolves. In the water, you would see various crocodile-like animals, among them large amphibians and distant relatives of true crocodiles. Later in the Mesozoic, as Pangea gradually broke into separate landmasses, more diverse forms of animal life began to appear.

TRIASSIC MEAT-EATERS

Small meat-eating dinosaurs of the Triassic period hunted insects, such as cockroaches and dragonflies, and frogs. Larger carnivores, such as *Zanclodon*, would have gone in search of bigger prey, such as mammal-like reptiles and even early mammals.

Zanclodon

Herrerasaurus

Procompsognathus

Saltopus

THE JURASSIC PERIOD

Changes occurred very gradually during the Jurassic period. In the early Jurassic, the world—as it had been in the Triassic—was still generally warm and arid, especially near the equator, and there was little difference in land animals from one region to another. This changed, however, as the period progressed.

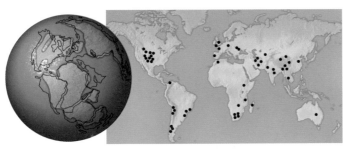

MOVING APART
During the Jurassic, the single landmass of Pangea broke up to form Laurasia in the north, and Gondwana in the south.

JURASSIC DINOSAUR SITES
This present-day map shows those parts of the modern world in which fossils of Jurassic dinosaurs have been found.

Drifting apart In the Jurassic period, definite change was under way. Even at the very end of the Triassic, the slow but inexorable breakup of Pangea had started. The ancestral Atlantic Ocean began to form as North America separated from Europe and Africa. By the end of the Jurassic, we see separations, not only between the Americas and the Old World, but also between the world's northern and southern landmasses. What would later become the southern continents—South America, Australia, Africa, Antarctica and India—were to remain in contact for the rest of the Jurassic and for much of the Cretaceous. The broad landmass they formed is now referred to as the southern continent of Gondwana. The northern part of the former Pangea is now called Laurasia.

RISING IN DEFENSE
A long-necked *Diplodocus*, disturbed while browsing on plant matter with other members of a herd, rears up to defend itself against a predator. Its clawed front feet and long, lashing tail are ready for battle.

THE JURASSIC PERIOD continued

JURASSIC LANDSCAPE

Thanks to a generally warmer and more humid climate, more expansive forests grew in the Jurassic period, and plant groups that were present in the Triassic diversified greatly.

Expanding oceans Scientists generally agree that both the North and South poles were completely free of ice during the Jurassic. It also seems probable that during periods of increased tectonic activity there was some slight expansion in some parts of the oceanic crust. Therefore, the lack of polar ice increased the amount of water in the oceans, and the expanding sea floor dispersed the water more widely. As a result, sea levels around the world rose during the Jurassic, and large sections of the continents were flooded. This in turn added to the breakup of landmasses that tectonic activity was already causing; expanses of water now separated what had previously been continuous stretches of land.

Warm and humid The world was uniformly warm during the Jurassic, although it was slightly cooler than it had been throughout the Triassic period. In contrast to the variable seasons that occurred

Camptosaurus

Allosaurus

Stegosaurus

Coelurus

during the Triassic, seasons during the Jurassic probably varied only slightly. However, after the early Jurassic, climatic differences probably became rather more accentuated, largely because of the increased fragmentation of the landmasses. Although everywhere was warm, some areas became more humid and received greater rainfall than others.

Flowers and plants There were probably still no flowering plants during the Jurassic. It seems likely that potentially flower-bearing plants did not evolve flowers until the late Cretaceous. Forests, however, flourished and spread in the warm, wet Jurassic climate. They continued to be dominated by needle-bearing conifers, cycads, tree ferns and ginkgoes.

JURASSIC DINOSAURS

The Jurassic saw the appearance of a wide range of both meat-eating and plant-eating dinosaurs of greatly differing sizes. *Coelurus*, a theropod, grew 7 feet (2 m) long, while the plated plant-eater *Stegosaurus* grew to a length of 30 feet (9 m).

THE CRETACEOUS PERIOD

During the Cretaceous, which lasted more than 80 million years, more dinosaur species evolved than in the Triassic and Jurassic periods combined. In the Cretaceous, the giant plant-eaters all but disappeared and were replaced by smaller species such as *Triceratops* and the hadrosaurs.

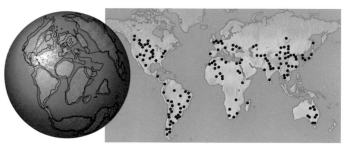

CHANGING WORLD
The continuing breakup of the world's landmasses during the Cretaceous led to a greater diversification of species.

DINOSAUR SITES
Cretaceous dinosaur sites are much more numerous than dinosaur sites from the Triassic and Jurassic periods.

Climate The early Cretaceous was warm. Winters were mild and dry, and most of the rain fell in summer. Later, summers became hotter and winters were colder in the temperate and polar regions.

Flowering plants Flowering plants emerged early in the period, and by the end of the Cretaceous they were very diverse. Some groups, such as water lilies, had appeared, but there were no grasses until after the Cretaceous.

A cascading effect The arrival of flowering plants had an effect on other groups of organisms. There is evidence that complex relationships existed early in the period between plants and insects. Bees, for example, relied on plants for food, while the plants relied on insects for pollination.

WHITE CLIFFS
The Seven Sisters Cliffs in East Sussex, southern England, are formed from the white chalk deposits that were laid down during the Cretaceous period.

THE CRETACEOUS PERIOD continued

FIRST FLOWERS
Cretaceous plant-eating dinosaurs cleared areas of conifers and cycads, creating spaces that were conducive to the development of flowering plants.

Dinosaur diversity Sauropods continued to be diverse early in the Cretaceous, but the numbers of these huge dinosaurs declined slowly during the period. By the later Cretaceous, the dominance in the northern continents had shifted from the sauropods to the ornithopods and ceratopsians. The ceratopsians, a group of horned dinosaurs, were among the last dinosaurs to evolve. Some scientists believe that the changes in the dinosaur fauna, and its increasing variety, were a response to the expanding diversity of flowering plants in the local flora.

Change and cataclysm Sea levels rose and fell a number of times during the latter half of this period. North America was cut almost in half by a shallow sea. Western North America was connected to eastern Asia, and some groups of dinosaurs were unique to these regions. Today's landmasses of South America, Antarctica, Madagascar and India all shared unique groups of dinosaurs during the Cretaceous. Dinosaurs also existed in what is now Australia during the Cretaceous. Some of these seem to have had large eyes, specially adapted for night vision.

Cataclysm At the end of the Cretaceous period, sea levels were falling, temperatures were dropping and there was extensive volcanic activity. As well, a large asteroid or comet hit the Earth. Any or all of these could have played a part in the extinction at this time of half of the world's animals, including all of the Mesozoic dinosaurs.

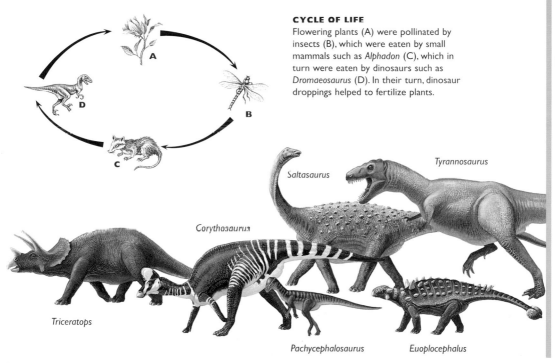

CYCLE OF LIFE

Flowering plants (A) were pollinated by insects (B), which were eaten by small mammals such as *Alphadon* (C), which in turn were eaten by dinosaurs such as *Dromaeosaurus* (D). In their turn, dinosaur droppings helped to fertilize plants.

A

B

C

D

Tyrannosaurus

Saltasaurus

Corythosaurus

Triceratops

Pachycephalosaurus

Euoplocephalus

DINOSAURS' CONTEMPORARIES

During the Mesozoic era, dinosaurs ruled the land, marine reptiles dominated the sea and flying reptiles, called pterosaurs, glided through the skies. Pterosaurs were the first animals with backbones to take to the air.

JURASSIC PTEROSAUR
Rhamphorhynchus, a pterosaur of the late Jurassic, had a distinctive long tail. This animal grew to about the size of a modern-day seagull.

FOSSIL
This *Rhamphorhynchus* fossil is one of the many superb pterosaur fossils to be unearthed from the late Jurassic site at Solnhofen, in Germany.

Sea life In the Mesozoic world, the waters were populated by a number of sea reptiles such as plesiosaurs, pliosaurs, marine turtles and crocodiles, as well as by fish, including the early ancestors of modern sharks.

Plesiosaurs and pliosaurs

Ichthyosaurs and sauropterygians were ancestors of later marine reptiles. They appeared in the Triassic and their dominance as marine predators lasted for more than 100 million years. The teeth and jaws of ichthyosaurs were well adapted to their diet of fish and cephalopods. The plesiosaurs were the descendants of one of the sauropterygian groups, called the nothosaurs. The plesiosaurs appeared very early in the Jurassic period. In these animals, the four limbs of their terrestrial ancestors became paddles that they used for swimming through the water, and the tail was greatly reduced.

Some plesiosaurs had extremely long necks—the elasmosaurs of the Cretaceous had necks with more than 80 vertebrae. The head was small and could be moved quickly when catching prey such as fish. Pliosaurs, on the other hand, had short, flexible necks and massive, strong skulls, and were capable of handling much larger prey, which they attacked head on.

CRETACEOUS LIZARD
North American theropods in the Cretaceous fed upon early lizards such as *Polyglyphandon*, which grew to about the size of a present-day rabbit.

ANCIENT MAMMAL
Mammals, such as *Crusafontia*, were common during the Cretaceous. However, none of them grew any bigger than a modern cat. They were preyed upon by meat-eating dinosaurs.

DINOSAURS' CONTEMPORARIES continued

LARGE TURTLE
During the Cretaceous, some turtle species became very large. *Archelon* grew to 13 feet (4 m) long—about as big as an automobile.

In the air The first true vertebrate fliers, the pterosaurs, appeared in the late Triassic and survived right to the end of the Cretaceous. The earliest pterosaurs were crow-sized. Their jaws were filled with sharp teeth and they had long, slender tails. Later pterosaurs had shorter tails, were toothless, and, toward the end of the Cretaceous, some of them became extremely large.

On the land During the early Triassic, synapsids were the most diverse group of large-bodied vertebrates on land. Throughout the Triassic, synapsids became smaller and more mammal-like. The first true mammals, however, did not appear until the Jurassic and although small, they were probably diverse. A number of reptile groups were common throughout the Mesozoic. They included the ancestors of modern crocodiles and alligators as well as lizards. Lizards were very diverse during the Cretaceous. They included some large terrestrial predators. A particular group of legless lizards—the snakes—made their first appearance during the Cretaceous period.

IN SOUTHERN SEAS
Known from Queensland, Australia, *Kronosaurus* was a pliosaur of the early Cretaceous. It grew to more than 40 feet (12.5 m) long.

PLESIOSAUR FOSSIL
Plesiosaurs appeared in the early Jurassic and survived to the end of the Cretaceous. They were distant cousins of the dinosaurs.

BIG EYES
Ophthalmosaurus was a late Jurassic ichthyosaur. It had huge eyes, which suggests that it probably fed at night.

EARLY CROCODILE
Deinosuchus was an ancestor of modern crocodilians. It lived during the Cretaceous and grew to 49 feet (15 m) long.

THE END OF THE DINOSAURS

Dinosaurs dominated the landscape for most of the Mesozoic and, in a sense, they still live on in the birds, which are their direct descendants. However, the animals we usually think of as dinosaurs died out at the end of the Cretaceous.

SOURCE OF DESTRUCTION
At the end of the Cretaceous a lone *Triceratops* observes a possible source of its destruction—a massive meteorite strike that created an ongoing sequence of environmental devastation.

Uncertainty Just what caused the extinction of the nonavian dinosaurs is still hotly debated. Today there are very few places

SPACE TRAVELER
This meteorite, which is believed to have come to Earth from Mars, is 4,500 million years old.

where the Cretaceous–Tertiary (often called the K/T) boundary is preserved in a sequence of land or freshwater sediments. We have a good idea of what happened in the marine realm, but only a few dinosaurs—in the form of aquatic birds—lived in the sea. So we are forced to generalize from what the few K/T sites reveal and apply these theories to the whole world.

Mass extinction As far as we can tell, as much as 70 percent of species of marine organisms became extinct at the end of the

Cretaceous. We know less about what happened on land, but it is clear that all nonavian dinosaurs disappeared at this time. So too did the pterosaurs and many groups of smaller invertebrates.

Sudden or gradual? Some researchers have argued that the nonavian dinosaurs disappeared suddenly. Others suggest a much more gradual extinction. There is not enough evidence to resolve this. It does seem, though, that marine animals may have become extinct more rapidly than land animals.

The Age of Dinosaurs

DEATHLY LANDSCAPE

Landscapes such as Death Valley, California, were characteristic of much of the post-Cretaceous world.

MAMMAL SURVIVOR

Purgatorius was one of the numerous small mammals that survived the cataclysmic events that occurred at the end of the Cretaceous.

Possibilities Most paleontologists now believe in one or more of three major theories to explain the K/T mass extinction. All three theories have good evidence to support them. The first involves climatic changes that brought about rising sea levels. These could have resulted in increased fragmentation of terrestrial habitats, which in turn could have broken up large concentrations of animals, resulting in smaller populations, which would be more vulnerable to environmental changes. However, this seems unlikely to have brought about a sudden demise of land or sea animals. The second major theory involves extensive volcanic eruptions. Several parts of the world at the end of the Cretaceous were experiencing a huge amount of volcanic activity. The most spectacular evidence for this is the Deccan Traps, a massive set of flood basalts in India. The third, and most dramatic, theory postulates the impact of a comet or asteroid at the very end of the Cretaceous. Several lines of evidence—including certain elements and minerals found in boundary sediments—support such a theory. Also, scientists now believe they have found a crater caused by a huge impact at the end of the Cretaceous. It is in the Yucatàn Peninsula in Mexico, but it is buried deep underground.

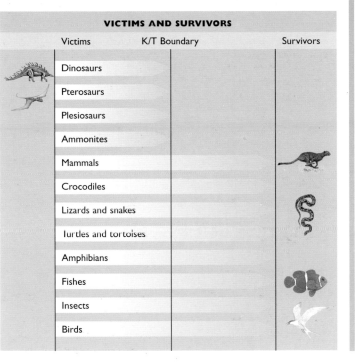

VICTIMS AND SURVIVORS		
Victims	K/T Boundary	Survivors
Dinosaurs		
Pterosaurs		
Plesiosaurs		
Ammonites		
Mammals		
Crocodiles		
Lizards and snakes		
Turtles and tortoises		
Amphibians		
Fishes		
Insects		
Birds		

PART TWO

ALL ABOUT DINOSAURS

DINOSAUR FEATURES

Almost everything we know about dinosaurs is based on bones, in many cases very fragmentary, that have been discovered and analyzed over more than a century and a half. They are the key to our understanding. It is through them that we can identify the features that distinguish dinosaurs from other animals, and it is by studying them that paleontologists have been able to reconstruct and theorize about the physical features of dinosaurs and the way they experienced and survived in their world.

FEATURES IN COMMON

Dinosaurs, like all other animals, are identified by the key features they have in common. In the same way that we recognize mammals because they have fur or birds by their feathers, we can recognize dinosaurs from their unique features.

JAWS AND TEETH

Even though it was not a reptile, *Dimetrodon* had jaws and teeth similar to those of many dinosaurs.

Looking at bones Because all our knowledge of dinosaurs comes from fossils of their skeletons, their unique features must be found in their bones. Similarly, different groups within the dinosaurs are recognized and classified by their bony features. The skulls of vertebrates contain two bones in the palate, called vomers. In dinosaurs, the vomers reach from the front of the snout back to the level of the holes in the skull in front of the eyes. In most other animals, the vomers are not this long.

Front and back limbs In the shoulder blades, or scapulae, dinosaurs had a socket that faced backward where the arm attached. This feature was perhaps related to another on the upper arm bone (the humerus)—a long, low crest on the upper part that provided attachment for muscles. The hand had a fourth finger that contained no more than three finger bones (phalanges). The tibia (shin bone) on dinosaurs was far larger than the calf bone (fibula). The ankle bone (astralagus) had a process that reached up the leg and fitted into a notch on the tibia. The ankle was a simple hinge, and dinosaurs walked on long toes. Key features of both the front and back limbs of dinosaurs allowed the legs to swing backward and forward under the animal, thus providing a very efficient way of moving about.

DIFFERENT GAITS

A dinosaur's weight was supported easily by its straight legs, tucked under its body (left). As the body weight was balanced over the hips by the weight of the tail, some dinosaurs could move around on two legs and use their hands for grasping.

Some reptiles, such as crocodiles, have upright hind legs (right). As their bodies are off the ground, they can run for short distances with their legs under them.

EGG-LAYERS

It seems probable that all dinosaurs began life as embryos that developed in, and hatched from, eggs laid in nests by adult females.

The ancestors of the dinosaurs sprawled on all four legs like a lizard (left).

TWO TYPES OF HIPS

Paleontologists have divided dinosaurs into two major groups: the saurischian (or lizard-hipped) dinosaurs and the ornithischian (or bird-hipped) dinosaurs.

SAURISCHIAN HIP
The ilium (purple) supported the leg muscles, transferring leg movement to the rest of the body. The forward-pointing pubis (red) also helped support the strong leg muscles. The ischium (blue) supported muscles that carried the tail off the ground.

BUILT FOR STRENGTH
The hip structure of *Tyrannosaurus* was typically saurischian. The socket where the thigh bone (femur) attached to the hip is clearly visible in this reconstructed specimen.

Two types Some dinosaurs—the meat-eating theropods, the long-necked sauropods and the prosauropods—had a pubic bone (one of the major hip bones) that pointed forward. These dinosaurs were called lizard-hipped dinosaurs, because their hips were similar to those of lizards. Other dinosaurs had a pubic bone that pointed toward the rear and ran parallel to another hip bone (the ischium). These were called bird-hipped dinosaurs, because their hips bore a superficial resemblance to the hips of present-day birds.

Saurischian features Some other features, too, are unique to each group. Lizard-hipped dinosaurs had a grasping hand with the thumb offset to the other digits and a second finger that was longer than the others. The neck was long and flexible, curving in an S-shape. These features were modified beyond recognition in some of the more advanced saurischians. In sauropods, for example, the hand developed into an elephant-like foot for bearing the weight of the front of the animal, while in birds, the three remaining fingers on each hand fused into a complex bone that supported many of the wing feathers.

LIZARD-HIPPED
Allosaurus, a carnivore from the late Jurassic, was a saurischian. Its pubis pointed forward between the legs and with the other pelvic bones formed a triangle to support the leg muscles for fast running.

75

TWO TYPES OF HIPS continued

Ornithischian features Bird-hipped dinosaurs had only small teeth at the front of the mouth. However, in many species these teeth were lost and were replaced by a beak. They also had an extra bone (the predentary) at the front of the lower jaw. This bone supported the beak. Another feature of many ornithischian dinosaurs was the development of horns, spikes, plates, frills and a variety of other bone ornaments. These provided the dinosaurs with an array of defensive and offensive devices. These features may also have been useful in attracting mates. All ornithischians were plant-eaters, while saurischians counted among their numbers both herbivores and carnivores. Although all ornithischians are now extinct, saurischians survive to this day as birds.

CROCODILE HIPS
Present-day crocodiles and alligators have hip structures similar to those of the lizard-hipped (saurischian) dinosaurs, with which they shared common ancestors.

BIRDS' HIPS
The hips of modern birds look similar to those of bird-hipped dinosaurs, but birds evolved from lizard-hipped dinosaurs.

BIRD-HIPPED

Edmontosaurus had a typical ornithischian hip. The backward-pointing pubis allowed space for the large intestines that plant-eaters needed to digest their food.

ORNITHISCHIAN HIP

The pubis (red) pointed toward the rear and ran parallel with another hip bone, the ischium (blue). As with saurischians, the ilium (purple) supported the leg muscles.

SKELETONS AND SKULLS

The dinosaurs were a huge and varied group. This diversity is reflected in their skeletons, which show a variety of forms, ranging from the enormous frames that supported the sauropods—which included the largest animals ever to walk the Earth—to the delicate, elegant structures of the smallest dinosaurs.

SAUROPOD SKELETON
Camarasaurus was a large late Jurassic sauropod that grew to 59 feet (18 m) long. It had massive, pillarlike legs that helped carry its great weight and deep ribs to support a large stomach.

Common themes Despite the dinosaurs' diversity of skeletal forms, many common themes were replayed throughout their history.

Skeletal diversity The secret of the dinosaurs' success lies partly in their design. Their legs were held directly under the body, which allowed them to swing forward and backward and meant that dinosaurs avoided the sprawling, ungainly gait that is typical of many other reptiles. A number of groups, such as the theropods, also had hollow bones that provided strength and support, while keeping the animals' weight to a minimum.

Structural strength Sauropods also developed weight-reducing adaptations in their skeletons. Because of their immense size, their skeletons had to be as light as possible while still providing the strength needed to support their tremendous weight. There were parts of the skeleton where structural strength was more important than saving weight. Massive leg and arm bones held up the bodies of sauropods, ceratopsians, stegosaurs and ankylosaurs. Weight-bearing legs were held as straight as possible, improving their capacity to carry huge weights. Armor, spikes, plates and shields made of bone tended to make an animal heavy. It is no surprise that these features are found in dinosaurs that moved on all fours, where the extra weight could be distributed more evenly. Small theropods and ornithopods had lightly built skeletons and a great deal of movement at the skeletal joints. They also tended to have very long legs for their size, indicating that they were fast runners, able to duck and dive away from larger predators.

SKULL CONTRASTS

Ceratosaurus (above) was a late Jurassic predator that grew up to 20 feet (6 m) long. It had a strong lower jaw and a high, narrow skull. Both jaws had large cavities to make space for the animal's very large jaw muscles. *Ouranosaurus* (below) was an early Cretaceous plant-eater that grew up to 23 feet (7 m) long. Although its jaw muscles were weak, this dinosaur was an efficient plant-eater. As it closed its mouth, the bones of the upper jaw moved apart, breaking up and grinding food with bands of cheek teeth.

Dinosaur Features

ORNITHOPOD SKELETON

Hypsilophodon, an early Cretaceous ornithopod, was a lightly built gazelle-like bipedal dinosaur. It used its long, clawed fingers to grasp plant food or to support its body as it grazed. It had a fairly large brain and large eye sockets, indicating good eyesight.

Skulls Dinosaurs' heads were encased in bone, which is heavier than flesh or muscle. Because of this, the very large heads of some dinosaurs were extremely heavy.

Ceratopsian heads In the case of ceratopsians, the heavy, bony heads were an advantage, because the extra bone provided protection against both attacks from predators and injury during combat with rivals. The great weight of a ceratopsian skull was balanced on a short neck and supported by huge muscles.

Sauropod heads The heads of sauropods, on the other hand, were at the end of long necks. These heads had to be big enough to permit the animals to collect sufficient food, but small enough not to weigh down the neck. In some sauropod skulls, the weight was minimized by expanding

Triceratops *had a huge skull with a beak for breaking off plant matter.*

holes—known as "fenestrae"—in the skull, thus reducing the bone to thin struts and rods.

Theropod heads Theropods generally had large heads. These not only had to be as light as possible, but they also had to withstand the tremendous forces that were transmitted through the head when the animal bit into or struggled with prey. These skulls, therefore, also had large holes, but the bony struts that surrounded them were still very solid.

NOSTRILS
The hadrosaur *Corythosaurus* (above) had a crest on its skull and nostrils at the front of its snout. Like most sauropods, *Brachiosaurus* (below) had its nasal openings at the top of the head, in front of and above the eyes.

WARM- OR COLD-BLOODED?

There is at present a lively scientific debate about whether dinosaurs were, like present-day reptiles, cold-blooded animals or whether, like today's mammals and birds, they were warm-blooded. The question is, however, not really about whether a dinosaur's blood was hot or cold.

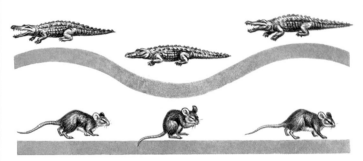

ACTIVE AND INACTIVE
Warm-blooded animals such as mice can be active all the time. Crocodiles and other cold-blooded animals must take in heat in order to become active.

Body heat On a hot day, a cold-blooded animal such as a crocodile may have a higher blood temperature than a warm-blooded mammal of a similar size. The relevant question is: Were dinosaurs able to maintain a constant body temperature, as mammals and birds do, or did their body temperature, like that of lizards, snakes and crocodiles, fluctuate in response to the environment?

Pluses and minuses There are both advantages and disadvantages in being able to maintain a constant body temperature. The main advantage is that a warm-blooded animal is always ready for action—night or day, hot or cold. This means that it is able to exploit habitats and conditions, such as near-freezing nights, that could not be tolerated by cold-blooded animals whose body temperature depends mainly on the environment. The main drawback of being warm-blooded is that it requires a great deal of energy. As a result of this, a warm-blooded animal needs to eat more. A warm-blooded lion, for example, must eat about twenty times as much as a cold-blooded crocodile of similar size. There are convincing arguments to suggest that dinosaurs displayed a variety of physiologies—that some could be recognized as truly warm-blooded while others were cold-blooded.

Theropods Theropods were the ancestors of warm-blooded birds, which some scientists argue is evidence that they, too, were warm-blooded. In addition, recent dinosaur finds in China show that small theropods had "hairy" coats, or even feathers, that would have helped trap heat inside the body.

HEAT REGULATOR
The large sail on the back of *Ouranosaurus* may have enabled this big plant-eater to regulate its body temperature.

WARM- OR COLD-BLOODED? continued

COLD HABITAT
Leaellynasaura, an early Cretaceous ornithopod from Dinosaur Cove in Victoria, Australia, lived and thrived well within the Antarctic polar circle, where few warm-blooded animals live today.

Smaller theropods could certainly have benefited from maintaining a constant body temperature, as this would have helped to keep them active while hunting. Several of these theropods, such as the dromaeosaurs, had slashing claws that are more typically associated with active, warm-blooded animals. Another argument for warm-blooded dinosaurs cites the small theropods and ornithopods that have been found at high-latitude sites such as Dinosaur Cove in Victoria, Australia, where Mesozoic winter temperatures were below freezing. Today, these environments are the domain of warm-blooded animals.

Evidence from crocodiles
Recent research has shown that "cold-blooded" crocodiles lose heat to the environment more slowly as

FOSSIL HEART

Some scientists believe that remains of *Thescelosaurus* include a fossilized heart, which is more like that of a mammal than the heart of a reptile. Others think the heart is simply a concretion—a deposition of minerals.

they grow. Increasing bulk, then, seems to act as a heat trap. If this applied to dinosaurs, the largest of them would sometimes have needed to shed heat absorbed from the environment or generated by moving muscles or digesting food. Long necks and tails, such as those of sauropods, could have helped with this by increasing the surface area relative to the mass of the animal. Plates, spikes and sails could also have helped to drain heat from the body. This may explain the function of the plates of the stegosaurs, or the sails on the backs of dinosaurs such as *Spinosaurus* and *Ouranosaurus*.

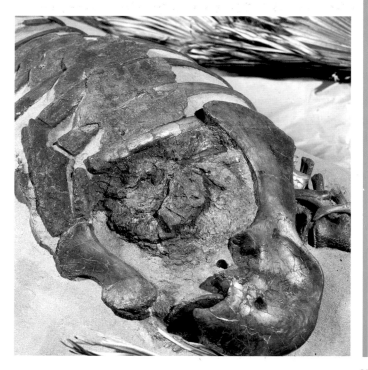

85

BRAINS AND SENSES

Like most soft tissue, brains, nerves and the sensory systems of dinosaurs have not fossilized. But we can learn a lot about what they were like by studying the bones that encased dinosaurs' brains, eyes and ears.

Brain space A dinosaur's brain is surrounded by bones that approximate the size and shape of the brain. The hole that is left by the brain can be filled with matrix or plaster to produce a copy, or "endocast," of this brain space. One problem with this is that to get at the endocast, the skull needs to be pulled apart. This could cause irreparable damage to the precious skull. Nowadays, Computer Assisted Tomography (CAT) scans, where the skull is X-rayed in three dimensions, can be used to analyze the brain spaces of dinosaurs.

Misconception It was believed that dinosaurs had a relatively small brain for their size. However, dinosaur brains were proportionally the same size as those of modern reptiles or amphibians.

Intelligence In animals, brain size in relation to total body size is an important factor in determining intelligence. Large plant-eaters, for example, had tiny brains relative to their body size. These giants, however, would not have needed a great deal of intelligence to find and consume their plant food.

BIG AND SMALL
The brain of *Iguanodon* (left) was particularly small in relation to its body size. A present-day rhesus monkey (right) has a relatively much larger brain, and is therefore significantly more intelligent.

HEAD TUBES

There are several theories about the function of the complex series of passages in the huge crest of a male *Parasaurolophus*. However, it seems likely that this crest may have served as an olfactory organ.

BRAINS AND SENSES continued

BRAIN SCAN
This Computer Assisted Tomography (CAT) scan of a *Tyrannosaurus* brain case is housed in the Field Museum in Chicago, USA.

Carnivores' brains The plant-eater *Iguanodon* had a body the size of a bus and a brain that was minuscule. The meat-eating *Deinonychus*, by contrast, had a much larger brain and a body the size of a large dog. Theropod dinosaurs needed greater brain power in order to locate, trap and catch their prey. The cerebrum, or "thinking" part, of a dinosaur's brain was smaller than that of a mammal. Dinosaurs, therefore, would have been slower than modern dogs or monkeys to learn new things.

Senses Theropods generally had well-developed eyes that included a ring of bone—the sclerotic ring—within the eye. In addition, the part of the brain that dealt with vision was larger than in other dinosaurs. This suggests that meat-eaters relied on sight as a primary sense for locating prey. Some plant-eaters, such as the pachycephalosaurs and the ornithopods, appear to have depended on a keen sense of smell in order to detect predators at a distance.

Nasal passages Both hadrosaurs and ankylosaurs had convoluted pathways for the air passages as they passed through the skull. The most extreme example of this is *Parasaurolophus*. The passages in its crest could have been sounding instruments, or they may have been lined with olfactory cells that gave their owners a very keen sense of smell. Yet another theory claims that they served to bring warm air into the lungs, to trap moisture from exhaling air or even to help keep the brain cool.

LARGEST BRAIN
Troödon had the largest brain for its size of any nonavian dinosaur. It was probably as intelligent as many modern-day ground birds. This intelligence helped it succeed and survive as a swift-moving hunter.

SMALLEST BRAIN
Stegosaurus had the smallest brain for its size of any dinosaur—or, indeed, of any known terrestrial vertebrate. Even though this dinosaur grew almost 30 feet (9 m) long, its brain was only the size of a walnut.

EATING AND DIGESTION

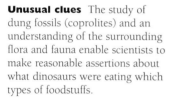

Several lines of evidence give us clues to the nature of dinosaur diets. Fossils of teeth, claws and jaws indicate food preference, while the occasional fossil with preserved stomach contents provides direct evidence of what a dinosaur was eating.

Unusual clues The study of dung fossils (coprolites) and an understanding of the surrounding flora and fauna enable scientists to make reasonable assertions about what dinosaurs were eating which types of foodstuffs.

Carnivores Theropods typically had long arms with sharp, curved claws that allowed them to grab their prey and rip at the flesh with rows of slashing teeth. Hunting in packs, the large Jurassic theropod *Allosaurus* probably preyed on animals ten times its size. It may

have overcome these beasts by ambushing them, slashing at them, then withdrawing until the prey was weakened by blood loss. It may also have fed on the young of large sauropods or attacked more modest-sized stegosaurs and camptosaurs.

Smaller theropods The smaller theropods had flexible skeletons that would have allowed for greater agility. Some of these would have either chased after smaller animals or formed groups to attack larger prey. The exceptions among the

theropods were the tyrannosaurs, which had puny arms. However, to compensate for this, they had particularly large mouths and the most powerful bite of any known animal, past or present.

LOOKING INSIDE
The huge plant-eater *Apatosaurus* fed on tough plant matter. After this food was broken down in the gizzard, with the help of gastroliths, nutrients were absorbed through the walls of the large and small intestines, and solid waste and urine were expelled through the cloaca.

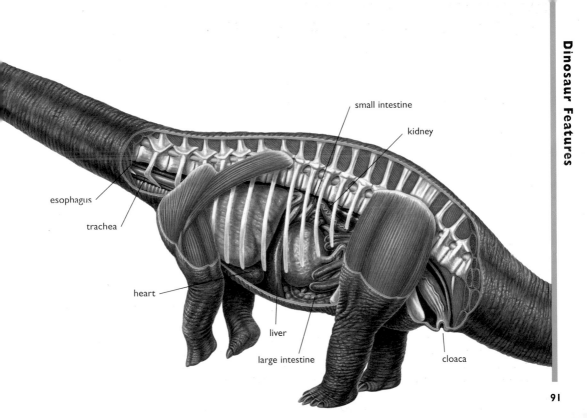

small intestine

kidney

esophagus

trachea

heart

liver

large intestine

cloaca

EATING AND DIGESTION continued

Herbivores The conifers, cycads, ferns and other kinds of tough vegetation that grew throughout most of the Mesozoic were both lacking in nutrients and relatively hard to break down. Plant-eating dinosaurs employed a number of strategies in order to deal with these problems, most of which involved the processing of large quantities of food. Sauropods stripped and swallowed plant matter largely without processing it in the mouth. While they could thus take in vast amounts of food, they had to break it down to retrieve the scarce nutrients. They appear to have done this in a huge vatlike pre-stomach, or gizzard, where the incoming food could be stewed and brewed into a nutrient soup. This process was helped by "gizzard stones," or gastroliths, that were held in the gizzard. These were ground together by the action of the stomach muscles and helped stir up the brew.

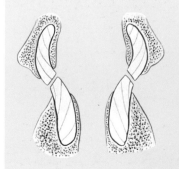

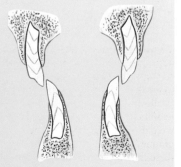

PREPARING FOOD

(left) The large duck-billed dinosaur *Edmontosaurus* stripped leaves off plants with its wide, flat beak, then used the batteries of grinding teeth at the back of its mouth to crush these leaves into a paste before swallowing it.

(right) The ceratopsian *Styracosaurus* snapped leaves off trees and bushes with the sharp, narrow beak at the front of its mouth, then used the rows of scissorlike teeth at the back of its mouth to snip these leaves into small pieces.

Dung fossils, or coprolites, probably from the plant-eater Titanosaurus, display remnants of plant matter.

ones. Advanced ornithischians took this technique to its limit, evolving batteries of very tightly packed teeth that functioned like a single grinding plate. These batteries grew continuously throughout the animal's life and could contain hundreds of teeth. The teeth at the front of the mouth snipped off the plant matter for grinding in the back of the mouth.

Grinding teeth The ornithopods, pachycephalosaurs and ceratopsians used grinding teeth to break down the food before swallowing it. This process took its toll on the teeth, which quickly wore down. However, a number of times throughout their lives these dinosaurs could discard their worn-out teeth and grow new

Lost teeth Ornithischians lost the teeth at the front of the mouth relatively early in their evolution. They replaced these with a sharp, birdlike beak. These animals appear to have had cheek pouches that prevented food from falling out while it was being chewed. Ridges of bone around the mouth that were probably supports for the cheeks have been observed in several of these dinosaurs.

GIZZARD STONES

While he was excavating the skeleton of the huge sauropod *Seismosaurus*, David Gillette noted and recorded the position of more than 240 gastroliths, most of them the size of apples, associated with the specimen. Most of these were collected just in front of where the stomach would have been. Others were scattered through other parts of the digestive tract.

DIFFERENT KINDS OF DINOSAURS

Like many other classes of animals, dinosaurs exhibited a huge diversity—of size, shape, physical features, diet and habits. This section looks at various categories of dinosaurs and examines the differences between them as well as the often marked variations between the animals within each group. It also looks at what is now a well-established evolutionary link between the dinosaurs of the Mesozoic period and present-day birds.

MEAT-EATERS

The meat-eating dinosaurs are all within one group, known as the theropods. Some of the earliest known dinosaurs are thought to have been theropods, giving them the longest history of any dinosaur group.

EARLY THEROPOD
Herrerasaurus was an early theropod from the late Triassic that grew to more than 6 feet (2 m) long. It hunted smaller animals, including, perhaps, other small dinosaurs.

Theropod features Most theropods were lightly built with large heads. They usually had bladelike teeth, often with serrated edges. Long, slender legs gave them greater speed than most other animals; they were all bipedal. Typically, they had long, curved claws that tapered to spiked tips, especially on the hands. They also had hollow bones, a feature that would help birds, their descendants, take to the air and fly.

Skull and vertebrae Another common theropod feature was some development of air pockets or pneumaticity of the skull and vertebrae. They had at least five vertebrae connected to the hip, and an extra joint in the mandible that allowed the jaws to flex sideways in order to accommodate large pieces of food.

Types of theropods Because theropod fossils tend to be rarer than those of their plant-eating relatives, and their types are more diverse, we know less about their interrelationships than we do of other dinosaur groups. Theropods can be divided into two basic groups—the ceratosaurs and the tetanurans. Ceratosaurs are known almost exclusively from rocks of the late Triassic and early Jurassic, although some of the theropods from the late Cretaceous of Africa and South America may also be from this group. Typical of the ceratosaurs were dinosaurs such as *Dilophosaurus* and *Coelophysis*. They had four functional fingers on each hand, and clawed toes on their feet. Tetanurans are the other main theropod group. They had no more than three functional fingers and a foot with three large toes plus a smaller one on the inside of the foot.

TOOTHLESS MEAT-EATER
Some theropods did not have teeth. Instead, they had sharp, narrow beaks. *Gallimimus*, a late Cretaceous tetanuran, probably fed on insects, small animals or eggs that it could swallow whole.

EGG THIEF?
Oviraptor, a late Cretaceous tetanuran, was long thought to feed on other dinosaurs' eggs. It now seems more likely that the eggs it was found near were its own.

97

MEAT-EATERS continued

CHEEK TEETH
Tyrannosaurus had 12 huge teeth in each side of its jaws.
The teeth were shaped more like serrated bananas than
the steak-knife shapes seen in most other theropods.

Carnosaurs Carnosaurs were a
group of (mostly) large tetanurans
that included dinosaurs such as
Allosaurus and *Sinoraptor*. This
group has changed significantly
in recent years. Originally the
carnosaurs were grouped together
based solely on their large size, but
some former members, such as
Tyrannosaurus, the largest of them
all, are now no longer thought to
be carnosaurs.

Coelurosaurs Most coelurosaurs
were Cretaceous tetanurans and
included such giants as the mighty
Tyrannosaurus and all its closest
relatives. Some of the stranger
coelurosaurs included the crested
oviraptors, the ostrichlike ornithomimosaurs and the slashing
dromaeosaurs. Ornithomimosaurs
and oviraptors were virtually
toothless. Dromaeosaurs had very

birdlike skeletons as well as a retractable claw on the second toe that could inflict severe wounds on their prey. Theropods were the major carnivores of their times. Some of them seem to have been social animals that lived in groups of several individuals. Fossil finds, however, suggest that many meat-eaters lived alone.

TINY HUNTER

Compsognathus, a late Jurassic tetanuran, was one of the smallest of all dinosaurs. It was an agile hunter of smaller animals. One specimen was found with the bones of a tiny lizard in its stomach cavity.

HUGE HUNTER

Growing about 40 feet (12 m) long, and weighing about 7 tons (7 tonnes), *Tyrannosaurus* was one of the largest terrestrial predators that has ever lived.

PLANT-EATERS

Plant-eating dinosaurs came in an extremely wide range of body types. There were both the ornithischian and saurischian plant-eaters, as well as bipedal and quadrupedal ones.

CHEEK POUCHES
Othnielia, from the late Jurassic, had cheek pouches to store food so the plant matter it ate could be chewed thoroughly later on.

Saurischians There are two categories of saurischian plant-eaters—the prosauropods and sauropods. The earlier prosauropods ranged from medium and quite small to large animals with long necks and tails, small heads and large bodies. They were all quadrupedal. Sauropods probably had a prosauropod ancestor, and ranged in size from large to extremely large. Their necks and tails were generally longer than those of the prosauropods, their heads were smaller, and their bodies more barrel-like. Both prosauropods and sauropods relied for their survival on processing large amounts of low-quality food, which they swallowed whole, without chewing. Gizzard stones (gastroliths) in their stomachs helped to crush the very tough fibers of this plant matter.

CHANGING DIETS

The food available to plant-eating dinosaurs changed throughout the Mesozoic, as new varieties of plants evolved along with new species of dinosaurs. Triassic dinosaurs ate horsetail ferns that grew as big as trees. Jurassic dinosaurs ate even tougher vegetation, including pine cones and cycad fruits. Cretaceous dinosaurs had access to flowering plants, including magnolias.

horsetail ferns

magnolia

pine cone

GASTROLITHS

These stones processed the food of sauropods, such as *Saltasaurus*. The gastroliths were ground together by the muscular action of the stomach.

PLANT-EATERS continued

Ornithischians While the ornithischian dinosaurs represent a great diversity of dinosaur types, all of them were plant-eaters. Within this group are the shielded thyreophorans, including stegosaurs and ankylosaurs; the ornithopods, including the iguanodontids and the hadrosaurs; and also the marginocephalians, a category that included the ceratopsians and the pachycephalosaurs. Thyreophorans all had some form of bony armor on their backs. Ornithopods take their name (meaning "bird-foot") from the three-toed, birdlike feet of many members of the group. The group was characterized by animals that had relatively large heads, moderately long necks and long hind legs. They could travel on all four legs, or rise up on two if more speedy or agile movements were required. There is also a trend in this group of dinosaurs to develop bony struts ("ossified tendons") along the back, over the rump and down the tail. The marginocephalians were a group that all featured some form of bony growth around the margin of the head. Pachycephalosaurs were covered with a series of lumps and bumps, while their cousins, the ceratopsians, evolved a bony frill that, in some later animals, extended well back over the shoulders. Pachycephalosaurs

---

TOUGH FOOD

Almost everything we know about dinosaurs—what they looked like, how big they were, how they moved and the kinds of food they ate—comes from their fossilized remains, especially their bones and teeth. Other fossils, too, provide valuable clues. Fossils of plants, for example, that have been dated to different periods tell us what plant food was available to plant-eaters at various times. Fossils of cycads, ginkgoes, conifers and ferns have been dated back to the Triassic. This very tough vegetation would have been the staple diet of the early plant-eating dinosaurs, who lived in a world in which flowering plants did not yet exist.

conifer pine

cycad

ginkgo

TEETH

Heterodontosaurus, an early Jurassic ornithopod, had small cutting teeth in the front upper jaw and a horny beak on the lower jaw. As well, it had two pairs of large tusks.

FOSSIL TRACK CLUES

Thanks to fossil tracks, we know that *Iguanodon*, while mainly quadrupedal, could also move on its back legs.

were all bipedal and could be readily identified by their thick, bony heads, which were often ornamented with lumps and spikes of solid bone. Ceratopsians were mostly quadrupedal and had particularly large heads. The size of the head was further exaggerated by the neck frill and horns and spikes on the face.

LONG-NECKED DINOSAURS

Brachiosaurus, Diplodocus, Mamenchisaurus and Apatosaurus are four of the best-known of all dinosaurs. They were also some of the largest animals that have ever lived on the Earth.

Sauropods Members of the class Sauropoda—known generally as "sauropods"—were characterized by very long necks, tiny heads, long flexible tails, compact barrel-shaped bodies and massive legs that were like sturdy pillars. The largest sauropod so far discovered was found by the American paleontologist David Gillette in the Morrison Formation in New Mexico. It was named *Seismosaurus*, which, appropriately, means "earthquake lizard." It was more than 140 feet (43 m) long and would have weighed as much as 10 modern elephants. Its skeleton took eight years to excavate. The sauropods evolved during the late Triassic and early Jurassic and were at their most diverse in the late Jurassic period. They became progressively more scarce during the Cretaceous, when their status

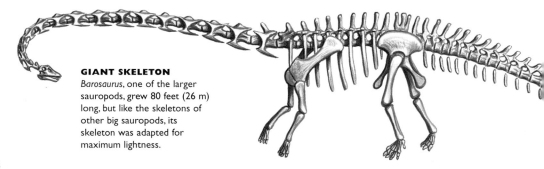

GIANT SKELETON
Barosaurus, one of the larger sauropods, grew 80 feet (26 m) long, but like the skeletons of other big sauropods, its skeleton was adapted for maximum lightness.

as dominant land animals passed to the large theropods and some ornithischian dinosaur groups. Some sauropods, however, evolved during the Cretaceous, and a few species survived right to the end of the age of the dinosaurs. One of these was *Saltasaurus*, a relatively small sauropod, which was found in Argentina in 1980.

MIGRATING HERDS

Fossil footprints and fossils of animals found in groups suggest that many sauropods lived in herds and may have migrated to find fresh food. There is evidence that the adults formed a cordon around their young, in order to protect them from predators.

LONG-NECKED DINOSAURS continued

Voracious eaters Sauropods were all plant-eaters, and they ate almost continuously. They needed to do this to take enough food into their small mouths to feed their large bodies. They ate mainly tough plant matter, such as pine cones, cycads and ferns, which they rapidly stripped from trees and bushes, swallowed whole without chewing and then slowly processed in their stomachs. They used their long necks to stretch high up into the tops of tall conifer trees or deep into dense forests. Although all sauropods moved about on four legs, some, such as *Barosaurus* and *Diplodocus*, had

RECENT FIND

Bones of a sauropod, *Superposeidon*, were discovered in Utah in April 2000. They suggest that this dinosaur may have been the largest land animal ever.

back legs that were longer than the front ones. They may have been able to rear up on these back legs to reach even higher—or, perhaps, as a show of aggression against would-be predators.

Light bones Sauropods had a number of weight-reducing adaptations in their skeletons. Despite, or more properly, because of, their immense size, their skeletons needed to be as light as possible, while still providing the strength that was needed to support their tremendous weight. Sauropods' neck vertebrae, for example, contained hollows and cavities, with many of the processes reduced to long bony struts. Edward Drinker Cope acknowledged this feature in 1877 when he named *Camarasaurus* ("chambered lizard") for the

LONGEST NECK
The longest neck of any known animal belonged to *Mamenchisaurus*. This neck, which was 49 feet (15 m) long and made up half the animal's total length, was not flexible, but this dinosaur could rear up on its hind legs to reach the tops of the highest trees.

hollow, boxlike nature of this animal's neck vertebrae.

High tails Until the 1980s, scientists thought that sauropods were lumbering beasts that moved about dragging their tails heavily along the ground. However, the lack of tail impressions on the ground accompanying any of the numerous examples of sauropod footprints led to a reappraisal. It was then realized that huge tendons that ran the entire length of a sauropod's body balanced the tail against the weight of the neck and enabled these animals to hold their tails out behind. As a result, museum displays around the world were changed accordingly.

LONGER NECK
Brachiosaurus's neck was 20 feet (6 m) long. Its reach was extended by the fact that this dinosaur's front legs were longer than its back legs.

DINOSAURS WITH ARMOR

Many plant-eating dinosaurs evolved special features that enabled them to defend themselves against predators or to fight other members of their species in order to win mates or establish territories.

Pros and cons Some were armed with spikes and horns; others were covered with plates and shields. A few combined all these features. One group—the pachycephalosaurs—had dome-shaped heads with thick, strong layers of bone. However, while this array of armor and weaponry was useful for attack and defense, it had the disadvantage of being

HORNS AND HOLES
The bony frill of *Styracosaurus* was fringed with sharp horns. It had two large symmetrical holes, or fenestrae, which greatly reduced its weight.

heavy, thus slowing the animal down and preventing a quick getaway. As well, the armored dinosaurs all had small brains, a further disadvantage when confronted with faster-moving, more intelligent predators.

Early examples All the armored dinosaurs were bird-hipped (ornithischians). Along with other ornithischians, armored dinosaurs diversified broadly during the Jurassic. One of the earliest to appear was the small stegosaur *Scutellosaurus*, from the early Jurassic of Arizona. Unlike later giants, *Scutellosaurus* was only lightly armored and reasonably fast-moving—even able to get around on two legs for short periods. During the late Jurassic period, some groups of armored thyreophorans, including some

SPIKY CERATOPSIAN

The aptly named *Styracosaurus* ("spiked lizard") was a spectacular-looking ceratopsian. It is possible that the elaborate horned frill was used more for courtship display than for defense.

stegosaurs, were common in North America, Eurasia and Africa. Stegosaurs had bony plates sticking out along their backs, and spikes at the end of their tails. *Stegosaurus*, which grew almost 30 feet (9 m) long, lived in the late Jurassic in North America. This dinosaur had one or two rows of back spikes that were shaped like big triangles, and two to six pairs of long, sharp spikes at the end of its tail. Contemporaries, and close relatives, of *Stegosaurus* were the 16-foot (5-m) *Kentrosaurus*, from Tanzania, and the lesser known 23-foot (7-m) *Tuojiangosaurus*, from Szechuan, in China.

DINOSAURS WITH ARMOR continued

LARGE BUT LIGHT
The frill of *Chasmosaurus* was much lighter than that of any of its relatives. The bony part of the frill consisted of little more than a framework for the two enormous openings within.

Ankylosaurs The ankylosaurs, which were common well into the Cretaceous, were another important group of armored dinosaurs. Their armor sometimes extended onto the flanks or even the belly. Of the two main groups of ankylosaurs, the nodosaurids, such as the late Cretaceous *Edmontonia*, from Alberta, Canada, were characterized by a boxlike head and bony armor that covered the neck, back and upper surfaces of the tail. Earlier nodosaurids are known from around the world in older rocks that date back to the late Jurassic. The ankylosaurids, the best known of which are *Ankylosaurus* and *Euoplocephalus*, are also from the late Cretaceous of Alberta. They had thick plates of bone and rows of spikes on their backs and sides, as well as a solid, double-headed club at the end of the tail.

Ceratopsians The ceratopsians, or horned dinosaurs, were the last group of ornithischians to evolve before the nonavian dinosaurs died out at the end of the Cretaceous. They were characterized by horns on the snout and head, and a large bony neck frill. *Triceratops*, which grew to 30 feet (9 m) long, was the largest member of the group, which also included *Centrosaurus* and *Protoceratops*. Because they lived for only a relatively brief period—about 20 million years— at the end of the Cretaceous, the ceratopsians did not achieve a worldwide distribution. However, along with the pachycephalosaurs, they spread out, living in vast herds across much of western North America and central and eastern Asia—landmasses that were still joined during the late Cretaceous period.

NODOSAURID

Polacanthus was a 13-feet (4-m) long nodosaurid. It had a double row of spines on the upper part of its body and a strong, spiked tail.

DISHES AND DAGGERS

Stegosaurus may have used its back plates for defense, or for heating and cooling. The spikes on its very flexible tail, however, were certainly used for self-defense.

PLATES AND SPIKES

Kentrosaurus, a stegosaur from Africa, had seven pairs of plates on its upper back and neck, and seven pairs of spikes on its back, hips and tail.

DUCK-BILLED DINOSAURS

The duck-billed dinosaurs, or hadrosaurs—members of the family Hadrosauridae—were a diverse group of plant-eating, duck-billed dinosaurs that lived in the late Cretaceous.

Hadrosaurs This family of large ornithopods are informally named for the wide, flattened front part of their mouths. This was covered in a horny, toothless beak that looked like the bill of a monstrous duck. Hadrosaurs were all plant-eaters—as a group, they were the most common and widespread plant-eating dinosaurs of the late Cretaceous. They used their "duck bills" to break off vegetation, which they then ground with the tightly packed teeth at the back of their mouths. Duck-billed dinosaurs are divided into two main groups—the hadrosaurines, such as *Maiasaura*

and *Edmontosaurus*, which lacked head crests; and the lambeosaurines, such as *Lambeosaurus*, *Corythosaurus* and *Parasaurolophus*, which had hollow bony crests on the tops of their heads. The size and shape of the lambeosaurines' crests varied greatly, both between the species and within the same species. This led some earlier paleontologists to overestimate the number of crested species. More recently it has become clear that these crests grew and changed as the animals matured and that some differences could be simply attributed to differences between the sexes of the same species.

LIVING TOGETHER

Flat-headed and crested hadrosaurs ate different sorts of plants, so like giraffes (which eat tree leaves) and zebras (which eat low-growing plants), they were able to live together because they did not threaten one another's food supply.

DUCK-BILLED DINOSAURS continued

FLAT HEAD
Edmontosaurus was a hadrosaurine dinosaur. Unlike the lambeosaurines, it had no bony crest on its head.

Moving and feeding The duck-billed dinosaurs walked and ran on their hind legs but leaned down on their shorter front legs to browse on plant matter. They fed on a wide range of vegetation, and this no doubt helped some of the species to survive as the late Cretaceous climate became drier, and different plants became more scarce. Lambeosaurines lived in the same area and at the same time. They were low-browsing, and had narrower snouts than the hadrosaurines. They may have fed on a narrower range of plants.

Spectacular finds The amazing find in Montana in 1978 of a huge nesting colony of *Maiasaura* shed fascinating new light on the nesting and rearing habits of this hadrosaurine dinosaur—and perhaps of hadrosaurs generally. The great size of the colony has suggested to some that hadrosaurs may have been strongly social animals. Such a theory seems to be supported, and extended, by the discovery, in Alberta, Canada, of a great number of skeletons of different hadrosaur species that were buried together by floods. These dinosaurs, it seems, may have shared the same habitat and lived together in large herds.

COLOR CHANGE

Some paleontologists believe that *Lambeosaurus*, and other plant-eaters, were able to change the colors of their skin at different times of the year to attract mates or to warn others off their territories.

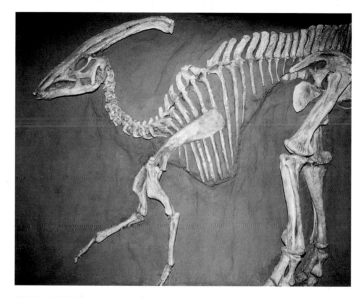

HEAD CREST

The head crest of *Parasaurolophus* was formed from long pieces of hollow bone that stretched from its snout over the top of its head. This is a cast of an almost complete skeleton that Levi Sternberg found in Alberta, Canada, in 1921.

TODAY'S DINOSAURS

Birds are the living descendants of the Mesozoic dinosaurs that became extinct 65 million years ago. Look at the footprints left by theropod dinosaurs, and you will see the imprint of three toes spreading out from the rest of the foot—just like the footprints of a present-day bird.

A dinosaur ancestry Today, a dinosaurian ancestry for birds is as well supported as a mammalian ancestry is for human beings. Seven skeletons of *Archaeopteryx*, the first known bird, have so far been found. This late Jurassic dinosaur preserves a number of features that made it a "missing link" between birds and other reptiles. The jaws have teeth and the tail is long and bony—both reptilian features—but, in at least some specimens, there are clear impressions of feathers on the body. The first specimen of *Archaeopteryx* was discovered in 1861, only two years after the publication of Charles Darwin's theory of evolution in *On the Origin of Species*, which gave the scientific community powerful evidence that species changed over a period of time. The birdlike *Archaeopteryx* was a critical discovery for scientists studying the origin of birds—modern birds are so modified for flight that it

HAIRY FIBERS
In 1996, *Sinosauropteryx*, meaning "Chinese lizard wing," was discovered in China. It had hairy fibers over much of its body. It is not yet clear if these fibers were feathers.

is difficult to link them to any earthbound group of animals. *Archaeopteryx* was a primitive enough bird to still retain many of the features of the nonavian relatives of birds.

LIMITED FLYER
It is almost certain that
Archaeopteryx could fly, but
probably only for short distances.
It is likely, however, that it would
dive from its perch to catch prey
such as insects and small reptiles.

TODAY'S DINOSAURS continued

Theropod to bird Like birds, all dinosaurs had an inturned femoral head and open hip socket. Again like birds, all theropods had thin-walled, hollow limb bones, complex air sacs in the skull and vertebral column, a three-toed foot and a hand dominated by the thumb, index finger and middle finger. As we look at smaller groups of theropods, the forelimb and hand become increasingly birdlike, with the complete loss of the fourth and fifth fingers and the development of a specialized wrist. The tail becomes stiffened and reduced in length, and in those theropods closest to birds, including *Deinonychus*, the pubis points down or back, not forward. From recent research, we know that many groups of theropods not only had collarbones but also true wishbones.

Feathers Until quite recently, only birds were thought to have feathers. In the 1990s, however, new finds in China have proved otherwise. *Sinosauropteryx*, from Liaoning province, preserved a halo of hairlike structures which, it is now thought, may be the precursors of true feathers. In two other Liaoning finds, *Caudipteryx* and *Protoarchaeopteryx*, the feathers are unambiguous—they

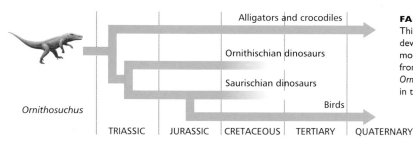

Ornithosuchus

Alligators and crocodiles

Ornithischian dinosaurs

Saurischian dinosaurs

Birds

TRIASSIC | JURASSIC | CRETACEOUS | TERTIARY | QUATERNARY

FAMILY TREE
This diagram shows the development of dinosaurs, modern reptiles and birds from a reptile ancestor, *Ornithosuchus*, which lived in the late Triassic.

have a central shaft (rachis) as well as fibers (barbs). This means that feathers, or their precursors, were clearly present on some groups of theropods and we can no longer simply draw a line that separates bird and theropod.

FOUND IN CHINA

Fossils of *Beipiaosaurus*, which was found in Liaoning, China, in the 1990s, preserved simple, short fibers, much like those of *Sinosauropteryx*.

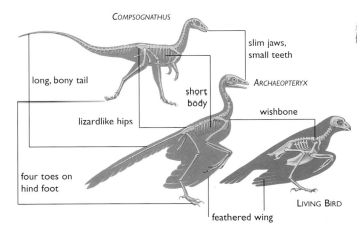

COMPSOGNATHUS

slim jaws, small teeth

long, bony tail

short body

ARCHAEOPTERYX

lizardlike hips

wishbone

four toes on hind foot

LIVING BIRD

feathered wing

DINOSAUR TO BIRD

Fossil records show a strong similarity between small bipedal theropods that ran upright on long, thin, hind legs, *Archaeopteryx* and living birds.

How Dinosaurs Lived

Since the 1920s, when the first dinosaur eggs and nests came to light, paleontologists have gained significant insight into how these animals reproduced and reared their young. Ongoing discoveries and analysis of fossil remains, including dinosaur trackways, have provided vital clues to how dinosaurs moved, interacted with each other and survived in their environment. This chapter provides an overview of various aspects of dinosaurs' behavior.

REPRODUCTION

As with all animals, dinosaur reproduction relied on mating between the sexes. While it is often difficult to identify the sex to which a dinosaur skeleton belonged, there are cases where skeletons of a particular species fall into two distinct forms. These differences were probably in some way associated with courtship, nesting and the rearing of young.

HOLLOW CREST
A male *Parasaurolophus* had a long, curved, hollow head crest that may have honked out a sound as loudly as a trombone. This could have helped this dinosaur to find a mate.

Body form There are two kinds, or morphs, of *Tyrannosaurus*: a heavy one and a lighter, more gracile, form. Evidence from the tail bones indicates that the smaller gracile form is the male. In many animal species females are larger, and this usually confers advantages in egg production or defense of the young.

Crests Differences in head crests among the hadrosaurs also suggest some differences between the sexes. In *Parasaurolophus*, for example, half the known adult specimens had a long crest, while in the rest the crest was much shorter. Perhaps the longer crest served as a mating device that allowed the males to boom out a mating call deeper and more striking than the calls the smaller-crested females were capable of.

FOUND IN MONGOLIA

The American paleontologist Roy Chapman Andrews (right) from the American Museum of Natural History and his assistant, George Olsen, are seen here excavating a nest of *Protoceratops* eggs in the Gobi Desert, Mongolia, in the early 1920s.

SAUROPOD EGGS

Sauropods laid their eggs, not in a nest, but in an arc across the ground. They laid the first egg, then moved their back legs around to lay the next egg, and so on.

HADROSAUR NEST

Hadrosaurs scraped out shallow holes for their nests. They lined the nests with vegetation to keep the eggs warm. They laid their eggs in a huge spiral.

REPRODUCTION continued

PROTECTION

An adult female *Maiasaura* sits protectively over her nest, ready to defend the eggs against possible egg thieves such as *Troödon*. *Maiasaura* nested in large colonies, with the nests situated about 23 feet (7 m) apart. This was enough space to prevent the adults from accidentally crushing each other's eggs.

Survival rates Dinosaurs seem to have laid large numbers of eggs during a season and, despite varying degrees of parental care, the survival rate of the young appears to have been rather low. Effectively, dinosaurs relied on the quantity of offspring for the perpetuation of a species. In contrast, present-day large mammals rely on carefully nurturing a small number of young.

Growing up Dinosaurs matured at quite a rapid rate. For example, a 10-inch (25-cm) long hatchling hadrosaur could grow to more than 6 feet (2 m) in a few years and attain an adult length of 26 feet (8 m) in a decade. It seems dinosaurs grew rapidly early in life, but their growth rates slowed dramatically at adulthood. While some dinosaurs stopped growing at an adult size, others seem to have continued to grow right throughout life.

Life span Dinosaur life spans are hard to calculate. They may have been as short as four or five years for small ones, such as *Troödon*, but as long as 150 years for the large sauropods.

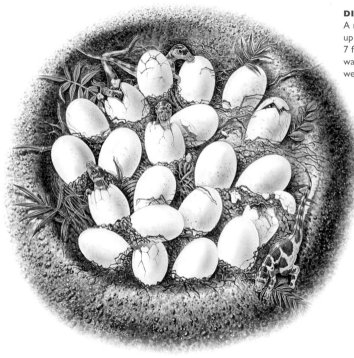

DINOSAUR NURSERY

A nest of *Maiasaura* eggs could contain up to 25 eggs. The bowl-shaped nest was 7 feet (2 m) wide, 3 feet (1 m) deep and was scooped out of mud. The hatchlings were about 18 inches (50 cm) long.

ON THE INSIDE

Inside the eggshell, a dinosaur embryo was enclosed in a fluid-filled amniotic sac. A yolk sac around this provided nourishment. A membrane called the chorion provided oxygen.

MOVING AROUND

One of the keys to the success of the dinosaurs was their posture. Even in the largest quadrupedal dinosaurs, the bulk of their weight was carried by the hind legs.

FLYING DINOSAUR
Archaeopteryx was a dinosaur, but was also the first bird. It was capable of powered flight, but probably only for very short distances, perhaps from one tree branch to the next.

Posture For many dinosaurs, their posture meant that they could rise up onto their hind legs, a stance that would have been very useful, either for defense or for display. In other dinosaurs, it meant two modes of carriage: all fours for energy-efficient movement, or two legs for fast getaways. Many dinosaurs were entirely bipedal, which freed the hands for grabbing prey or handling food.

Trackways The record of how dinosaurs moved is provided by their trackways. Trackways also supply us with unique information about dinosaur groupings and the structure of herds.

Small groups Larger theropods seem to have been solitary, or to have traveled in small groups. Smaller theropods favored larger groups. In one set of fossil tracks, in Queensland, Australia, dozens of small theropods gathered with a similar number of small ornithopods in a mixed group.

Larger herds Sauropods seem to have moved in groups of about a dozen of the same species, but of different ages. Larger ornithopods and ceratopsians formed vast herds, numbering hundreds or even thousands. These herbivores almost certainly migrated every year to seasonal pastures, a theory supported by trackway evidence.

MIXED GROUP
Small plant-eaters (left foreground) stick close to a large herd of long-necked sauropods as it migrates across the North American Jurassic landscape. Sharp-clawed theropods (right) shadow the herd, hoping to pick off a sick or injured animal.

MOVING AROUND: FAST AND SLOW MOVERS

Faster movers Standing on two long back legs, some dinosaurs, such as the ornithomimids, could sprint at considerable speed. The speed at which a dinosaur could move along can be measured partly by comparing the length of the leg below the knee (the shin) with the length of the leg above the knee (the thigh). The longer the shin, the wider the stride; and the longer the thigh, the more powerful the forward thrust. Ornithomimids and oviraptors had particularly long shins and relatively short thighs—even though their thighs were quite long in relation to the animals' overall size. Estimates of just how fast these dinosaurs could move have been derived from theoretical calculations that are based on the skeleton, and from measurements of fossilized trackways. It would

appear that fleet-footed theropods and ornithopods could reach speeds of at least 25 miles per hour (40 km/h).

Slower movers In general, the larger an animal, the more slowly it moves. Large theropods could probably move no faster than 9 miles per hour (15 km/h). Quadrupedal dinosaurs were still constrained by the "larger means slower" rule, but the ability to gallop and trot offered gaits that could be sustained for much longer periods of locomotion.

Amblers For sauropods and other very large dinosaurs, speed was probably never an option. Their sheer weight, their massive legs and the structure of their vertebrae would have limited them to a slow, ambling gait.

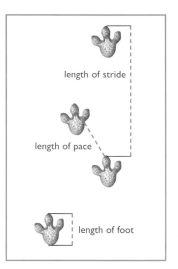

READING THE PRINTS
The length of a dinosaur's pace, the length of its stride and the length of its feet and legs allow scientists to estimate just how fast it could move.

FASTEST
Struthiomimus defended itself against predators by running at speeds of up to 31 miles per hour (50 km/h), balancing on its long, birdlike hind legs.

AMONG THE SLOWEST
The huge sauropods, such as *Diplodocus* (below) and *Mamenchisaurus* (above), were among the slowest moving of all the dinosaurs.

ATTACK AND DEFENSE

As for all animals, life for dinosaurs, whether plant-eating or meat-eating, consisted largely of finding enough food to survive while avoiding falling prey to other creatures.

BATTERING RAM
The skull of *Pachycephalosaurus* was able to withstand its charging attacks against other males, or predators.

Plant-eater strategies Plant-eaters evolved complex behavioral strategies and an array of defensive armaments to protect themselves from attack. Locked into an evolutionary arms race, and often facing keen competition for prey, predators evolved increasingly deadly weapons that they could bring to bear in attacking and subduing the animals they preyed upon. The sheer size of the largest dinosaurs, such as the sauropods, provided a defense against most predators. The tail of an adult sauropod was a weapon that could be wielded like a baseball bat and slammed into an attacker. The slender, more whiplike, tails of diplodocids could deliver deadly, stinging blows. But young sauropods were not protected by size and would have been easy prey. The defense of young sauropods probably came in the form of social structures, where adults could fend off attacks against their young by shielding them with their vast bodies.

130

DEADLY SWIVEL

Deinonychus used the sharp swivel claw on the second toe of each foot to kill its prey. It would leap into the air to kick, or balance on one leg as it slashed at the skin of plant-eaters.

HEAD TO HEAD

Two male *Pachycephalosaurus* butt heads like mountain goats to decide which of them will mate with a herd of females. Although protected by a solid dome of bone, one of them has become dizzy and is about to plummet to its death.

ATTACK AND DEFENSE continued

SPIKY SHIELD
Above *Triceratops*'s neck was a massive frill of solid bone and 3-foot (1-m) long horns that protected its head.

Built-in protection The horns of ceratopsians and the tail spikes of stegosaurs could have been used with great effect against predators. The spikes that covered ankylosaurs may also have been used as offensive weapons. Ankylosaurs had clubs at the end of their tails and a sheath of bony armor that could withstand bites and slashes. Display, too, could also be a useful defensive weapon. Ceratopsian frills and stegosaur plates may have flushed with color when the animal felt threatened, making the dinosaur look bigger or more intimidating.

Meat-eater strategies Some theropods were probably ambush predators. Hiding beside trails, they were ready to pounce on unsuspecting prey. Others could have hunted alone and in the open, their size and strength being decisive in any combat. Pack hunting was an effective tactic for some smaller predators. Some dromaeosaurs, such as *Deinonychus*, may have hunted in packs. Small groups of allosaurs, too, may have cooperated in attacks on sauropods.

Armed attackers Theropods were armed with cutting and slashing teeth and long, curved claws. Some claws, such as the huge hand claws of *Baryonyx*, appear to have grown to great lengths and probably had very specific functions. Similarly, the toe claws of the dromaeosaurs and troödontids were highly specialized and perfectly adapted for maiming or killing prey.

STABBING TAIL

Tuojiangosaurus used its muscular tail, which was armed at the tip with two pairs of sharp spikes, to defend itself against attackers.

BUILT FOR DEFENSE

With its studded bony armor and tail club, *Euoplocephalus* was better equipped than most dinosaurs to withstand attacks from predators.

MULTI-PURPOSE TAIL

Diplodocus used its very long tail for support when it reared up to crush a predator with its front legs, or swung it like a whip to blind or stun an attacker.

DINOSAUR SITES AND MUSEUMS

Dinosaur remains are often found in remote locations that are accessible only to professional paleontologists on well-equipped expeditions. Fortunately, there are numerous museums in many parts of the world that have extensive collections of fossils that are open to public view. Every year millions of people go to natural history museums to marvel at the earthly remains of dinosaurs—a visit that often provides the stimulus for an enduring interest in these wonderful creatures.

SITES AT A GLANCE

The following pages survey a selection of the world's most important dinosaur fossil sites, as well as museums that house and display significant collections of dinosaur fossils.

Paleontologists are always looking for new evidence of the dinosaurs and their world. Research teams of scientists comb the well-known sites as well as seek out fossils in previously unexplored locations. New sites, and fossil remains, regularly come to light and often attract widespread media attention. In the light of new discoveries, museums are constantly upgrading their collections and the way they display them. Museums are an invaluable resource for finding out more about the history of dinosaur finds, as well as about recent discoveries and ongoing research.

1. Smithsonian Institution, Washington DC, USA
2. American Museum of Natural History, New York, USA
3. Dinosaur National Monument, Utah, USA
4. Hell Creek, Montana, USA
5. Dinosaur trackways of the western United States, USA
6. Dinosaur Provincial Park, Alberta, Canada
7. Natural History Museum, London, UK
8. Musée National d'Histoire Naturelle, Paris, France
9. Holzmaden and Solnhofen, Germany
10. Las Hoyas, Spain
11. Institute of Vertebrate Paleontology and Paleoanthropology, Beijing, China
12. Zigong Dinosaur Park, Szechuan, China
13. Liaoning, China
14. Flaming Cliffs, Mongolia
15. Valley of the Moon, Argentina
16. Karoo Basin, South Africa
17. Lark Quarry, Queensland, Australia
18. Dinosaur Cove and East Gippsland, Victoria, Australia

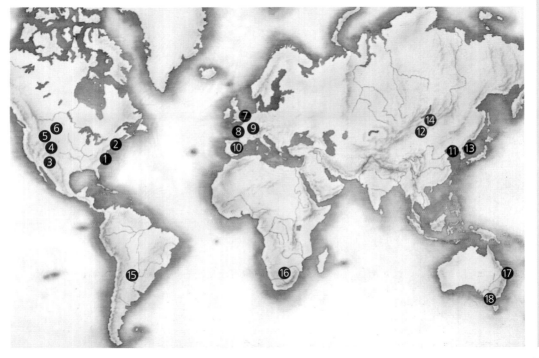

NORTH AMERICA

The United States and Canada have some of the
world's richest dinosaur fossil sites, as well as
numerous magnificent museum collections.

The Smithsonian Institution

Situated in Washington DC, the
Smithsonian Institution's National
Museum of Natural History
contains almost 50 million fossil
specimens, including more than
1,500 dinosaur specimens. The
museum's permanent exhibitions
include several mounted dinosaur
skeletons containing more than
50 percent original material.
Among them are *Albertosaurus*,
Allosaurus, *Ceratosaurus*, *Diplodocus*,
Triceratops and *Stegosaurus*. As
well, there are mounted casts of
the skeletons of a baby *Maiasaura*
and the South African dinosaur
Heterodontosaurus.

The American Museum of Natural History (AMNH)

This museum in New York City
contains the largest collection of
real dinosaur material anywhere in
the world. Teams of researchers
from this museum have been
conducting regular field trips since
1897. In 1902, an AMNH team,
led by Barnum Brown, discovered
the first *Tyrannosaurus* specimen
in the Hell Creek region of
Montana. The AMNH's new Halls
of Saurischian and Ornithischian
Dinosaurs, which were completed
in the mid-1990s, display more
than 100 dinosaur specimens,
most of which are entirely original.

BROUGHT TO LIFE
This lifelike reconstruction of
Stegosaurus is a popular exhibit in
the Smithsonian Institution's National
Museum of Natural History.

FOOTPRINTS
Fossil theropod footprints are clearly visible on this exposed rock ledge in the Morrison Formation in Utah.

BECKONING BANNER
A large dinosaur banner takes pride of place above the main entrance to the American Museum of Natural History in New York.

NORTH AMERICA continued

Utah The site of the Dinosaur National Monument was discovered in 1909 when Earl Douglas, of the Carnegie Museum in Pittsburgh, Pennsylvania, noticed a large sauropod skeleton eroding out of a sandstone ledge in part of the Morrison Formation in Utah. Visitors to this site can now see an exposed wall of sandstone that has been excavated to reveal some 1,500 dinosaur bones, estimated to be between 155 and 144 million years old. To date, 10 different genera of dinosaurs have been found at this site, making it the most diverse late Jurassic dinosaur locality anywhere in the world.

Montana The exposures at Hell Creek in Montana represent a sequence of late Cretaceous river deposits that have been dated to between 70 and 65 million years ago—the very end of the age of dinosaurs. The Hell Creek Formation has produced many splendid dinosaur specimens, including *Stygimoloch*, *Troödon*, *Albertosaurus* and *Torosaurus*.

FURRED FOSSIL-HUNTER
In 1902, Barnum Brown, an eccentric character who often wore a fur coat in the field, began looking for dinosaurs in the Hell Creek area. In that year he found the first, largely incomplete, skeleton of *Tyrannosaurus*.

RECENT DISCOVERY

This skeleton of *Thescelosaurus*, a small ornithischian dinosaur, was found in the Hell Creek Formation in Montana in 1993.

ANCIENT ROCKS

The upper layer of the sedimentary rocks at Hell Creek may date back to the Paleocene, the period following the extinction of the dinosaurs.

NORTH AMERICA continued

PREDATOR AND PREY
This reconstructed skeleton of *Albertosaurus* standing over a skeleton of *Centrosaurus* is on display in the Royal Tyrrell Museum in Alberta, Canada.

Trackways The western United States has a large number of significant trackway sites, ranging from the late Triassic to the late Cretaceous. Most of these occur in river, lake, shoreline and desert dunefield settings. Dinosaur trackways of the Triassic occur in the Chinle Formation of New Mexico, Arizona and Colorado. They comprise mainly the footprints of small coelurosaurs such as *Coelophysis*, and were left in riverside sediments. Late Triassic or early Jurassic dinosaur trackways occur in southern Utah, from the Warner Valley south of Zion National Park and near Tuba City, Arizona. The early Cretaceous Paluxy River trackways are exposed near Glen Rose in Texas. These are famous for insights they give into sauropod herd behavior.

Dinosaur Provincial Park
The extensive outcrops of the late Cretaceous Judith River Group along the Red Deer River in Alberta, Canada, have yielded a greater number of complete dinosaur specimens than any

other site on Earth. In 1955, an area of 28 square miles (73 km^2) of this land was established as Dinosaur Provincial Park. Field work in the park since the first dinosaur finds were made there in the early 1900s has yielded as many as 250 articulated dinosaur skeletons that represent some 36 different dinosaur species, including *Struthiomimus*, *Troödon*, *Dromaeosaurus*, *Euoplocephalus*, *Edmontonia* and *Lambeosaurus*.

ROYAL TYRRELL

The Royal Tyrrell Museum is situated near Dinosaur Provincial Park in Alberta, Canada. It contains many of the fossils collected within the park as well as specimens from many other parts of the world.

HORNED SKULL

The very well-preserved skull of the horned dinosaur *Pachyrhinosaurus* is one of the many specimens in the Royal Tyrrell Museum.

EUROPE AND BRITAIN

Museums throughout Europe and Britain contain a wealth of dinosaur fossils from many parts of the world, and a number of them are celebrated centers of paleontological research.

London For the past 200 years, London's Natural History Museum has housed the first dinosaur fossils ever found and described. As well, it has built up an enormous collection of fossils from around the world. Today, the museum holds some nine million specimens, including one of only seven known specimens of *Archaeopteryx*. Its dinosaur display was revised in 1991 to bring it up to date with the latest research into dinosaur biology and behavior.

Paris The Institut de Paléontologie, part of Paris's Musée National d'Histoire Naturelle,

DINOSAUR GALLERY
Dinosaur skeletons reconstructed in lifelike postures in the Galérie de Palinto in the Musée National d'Histoire Naturelle in Paris.

GRAND ENTRANCE
The cathedral-like facade of London's Natural History Museum in South Kensington. The present building was completed in 1881.

houses the large comparative anatomy collection of the French anatomist Baron Georges Cuvier (1769–1832), which includes the incomplete skeleton of the theropod *Streptospondylus*. The first dinosaurs collected from the rich Cretaceous sites of Madagascar are part of the institute's collection. These include the bones of the sauropod *Titanosaurus* and a piece of a domed skull that was originally identified as belonging to a pachycephalosaur but identified from later finds as an abelisaurid theropod. The museum also contains dinosaur specimens from Africa and Southeast Asia, as well as from various regions of France.

EUROPE AND BRITAIN continued

MARINE REPTILE
This Jurassic crocodilian, *Stenosaurus*, is one of the many beautifully preserved marine reptiles found at Holzmaden.

Germany The late Jurassic sites of Holzmaden and Solnhofen in Germany are famous for the fine state of preservation of their vertebrate fossils. Holzmaden has yielded the world's best fossils of marine reptiles, especially plesiosaurs and ichthyosaurs. Ichthyosaur fossils showing the outline of the entire animal, including its dorsal fins, have been preserved there. Some fossils, astonishingly, show young inside adult females. There is even one fossil of a female ichthyosaur giving birth. The vertebrate fauna of Solnhofen includes 54 species of fossil fishes, 28 kinds of reptiles and two dinosaurs—the complete skeleton of the little coelurosaur *Compsognathus* and the seven known specimens of the feathered dinosaur *Archaeopteryx*. Solnhofen has also produced many superb pterosaur fossils, including *Pterodactylus* and *Gnathosaurus*.

Spain The Las Hoyas site in Spain, in the Iberian mountain ranges of Cuenca Province, is an ancient lake deposit that has produced some of the world's best preserved bird and rare dinosaur fossils. So far only three dinosaurs have been found at Las Hoyas: some isolated bones of *Iguanodon*; an as yet undescribed sauropod; and a remarkably well-preserved partial skeleton of a primitive ornithomimosaur, *Pelecanimimus*, which shows impressions of skin and integumentary fibers. Las Hoyas, like Liaoning in China, is one of the world's most important fossil sites in providing evidence for the evolutionary link between dinosaurs and birds.

PTEROSAUR FOSSIL
Some pterosaur fossils from Solnhofen show exquisite preservation of these animals' delicate wing membranes.

FOSSIL SITE
The Solnhofen deposits are of finely layered lithographic limestone. This site is near the town of Eichstätt. The two other major sites are near the towns of Solnhofen and Kelhiem.

CHINA AND MONGOLIA

The Gobi Desert, in Mongolia, has been yielding exciting dinosaur discoveries since the 1920s. In recent times, discoveries in China have shed important new light on the evolution of birds from dinosaurs.

Flaming Cliffs This site in the Gobi Desert was discovered in 1922 by an American expedition led by Dr. Roy Chapman Andrews. Flaming Cliffs is the uppermost part of a 6 mile (10-km) escarpment of late Cretaceous sandstones known as Bayn Dzak. Within a day of finding the site, Andrews' team unearthed the first-ever dinosaur nest and a skull of *Protoceratops*. Further expeditions have discovered many new sites in the region. In 1993, an American expedition found the first articulated skeletons of oviraptorids brooding their eggs, some with embryonic dinosaur skeletons.

DESERT SANDSTONES

The rocks at Flaming Cliffs are made up mainly of poorly cemented dune and alluvial plain sandstones between about 87 and 72 million years old.

JOINT ENTERPRISE
Members of an American and Mongolian
joint expedition search for dinosaur
fossils in the Gobi Desert in 1991.

BADLANDS
Members of the 1922 American
Museum of Natural History expedition
to the Gobi Desert survey the
surrounding terrain from a cliff top
in the badlands at Urtyn Obo.

CHINA AND MONGOLIA continued

NEW BUILDING
In 1993 the IVPP in Beijing moved into a new, larger building, which has a three-story public area for fossil displays. Feathered Chinese dinosaurs and primitive birds from the early Cretaceous Liaoning sites are among the IVPP's most treasured specimens.

Chinese sites and museums

Quarries near Sihetun, in the province of Liaoning, in northern China, have recently become famous, thanks to their remarkable preservation of primitive birds and small dinosaurs with feathers and integumentary coats preserved. The discovery, in 1996, of the little dinosaur *Sinosauropteryx* caused a sensation because this was the first dinosaur to be found with a coat of what seemed to be fiber-like feathers. Other soft tissue preservation in the dinosaurs of Liaoning show the remains of gut contents, eggs inside oviducts and impressions of soft organs, such as the eye capsule. A large museum has recently been built on site to oversee excavations and house collections, and to display the most impressive specimens for visitors. Teams from the Institute of Vertebrate Paleontology and Paleoanthropology (IVPP) in Beijing are constantly scouring the far corners of China in their search for fossils. In the 1980s Professor Dong Zhiming from the IVPP, one of China's most celebrated paleontologists, discovered the Dashanpu Dinosaur Quarry in Zigong, in Szechuan Province. Today an impressive museum has been built above the site to house many of its important specimens as well as to show the excavations in progress. More than 8,000 fossil bones, including many complete dinosaur skeletons, have been excavated or exposed from the site.

LARGE THEROPOD
The large theropod *Gasosaurus* was excavated near Dashanpu, Zigong, China, between 1979 and 1981, and is on display in Beijing's IVPP museum.

SOUTHERN HEMISPHERE

South America, southern Africa and Australia were all part of the ancient southern continent of Gondwana. Searches in these regions have uncovered a range of Gondwanan dinosaurs from all three periods of the Mesozoic era.

Valley of the Moon The Valley of the Moon is a region in the north-west of Argentina in the province of La Rioja. It contains the oldest well-preserved dinosaur fossils anywhere in the world, as well as a range of other more primitive archosaurian reptiles that show evolutionary links to the first dinosaurs. The earliest dinosaurs were found in the Ischigualasto Formation, a succession of siltstones, sandstone and mudstones that have weathered into an alien-looking landscape of eroded gullies and steep cliffs. The fossils from the Ischigualasto Formation are dated to between about 226 and 220 million years ago. The first dinosaurs from the region were discovered by Dr. Osvaldo Reig. In 1960 he found the bones of the basal saurischians *Herrerasaurus* and *Ischisaurus* and he formally described them in 1963. Soon after that, the fragments of the first primitive ornithischian dinosaur, *Pisanosaurus*, were discovered here. During the 1988 field season, more complete material of *Herrerasaurus* was uncovered. Most dinosaurs found from this region are housed in the Buenos Aires Natural History Museum.

MADAGASCAN DINOSAUR
In 1993, a team of paleontologists found a perfectly preserved skull of *Majungatholus*, an abelisaurid theropod dating from the late Cretaceous of Madagascar. It was described in 1997.

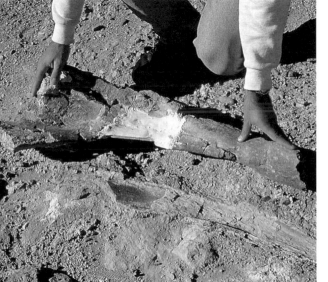

PIONEER FOSSIL-HUNTER
It was only after intensive field work in the Valley of the Moon in Argentina, that Dr. Osvaldo Reig discovered the first dinosaurs in the Ischigualasto Formation between 1959 and 1961.

ARGENTINIAN GIANT
Although it is known from only a few bones, these fossil remains suggest that *Argentinosaurus*, a recent discovery from Argentina, may have been the largest animal ever to have walked the Earth.

153

SOUTHERN HEMISPHERE continued

KAROO PIONEER
In 1838, Andrew Geddes Bain, a Scottish engineer, found the first fossil reptile in the Karoo Basin in South Africa. Since then, many different faunas, including some early Jurassic dinosaurs, have come to light there.

The Karoo Basin The Karoo Basin covers almost two-thirds of the surface area of South Africa. It is a thick sequence of sedimentary rocks laid down by large river systems, ranging in age from the middle Permian (the period before the Triassic) through to the early Jurassic (about 190 million years ago). The most notable sites for dinosaur and reptile fossils are in the early Jurassic Elliott Formation and the Bushveld Sandstone. Here, well-preserved remains of a number of early dinosaurs, such as the prosauropod *Massospondylus*, the small ceratosaur *Syntarsis* and the basal ornithischian *Heterodontosaurus* have been found. Theropod footprints have also been found in the Molteno Formation of the Karoo Basin. The Karoo Basin shows the most detailed record anywhere of the transition of life on land across the Permian–Triassic boundary, which, like the later Cretaceous–Tertiary boundary, was one of the Earth's major global extinction events.

Australian sites Lark Quarry, near Winton in Queensland, Australia, is one of the best preserved dinosaur trackway locations in the world. The site documents the activities of three different species of dinosaurs. More than 3,300 footprints, representing about 150 individual dinosaurs have been identified. These include footprints of a herd of small plant-eaters; a large number of small, predatory coelurosaurs; and a single, large carnivorous dinosaur. They are preserved in fine-grained sandstone, which is known as the Winton Formation and which is

RUGGED COUNTRY
The Lark Quarry site in Queensland, Australia, is situated in a scrubby, rugged landscape. The trackways there are on public display near the town of Winton.

dated between 95 and 90 million years old. The early Cretaceous coastal rocks of Victoria and the Otway Ranges of western Victoria, Australia, have so far yielded a diverse assemblage of vertebrates, including dinosaurs, pterosaurs, plesiosaurs, amphibians, turtles, fish and primitive mammals. Three hypsilophodontid dinosaurs—*Atlascopcosaurus, Qantassaurus* and *Leaellynasaura*—have now been named from these Australian sites. In 1994, the bones of an ornithomimosaur and a possible neoceratopsian were found, proving that these groups were not unique to the late Cretaceous period of the Northern Hemisphere.

PART THREE

DINOSAUR GUIDE

USING THE
DINOSAUR GUIDE

This guide gives a detailed
introduction to a wide range
of dinosaurs. Fossil finds have
provided vital clues about the
environments that dinosaurs
inhabited, as well their diet,
appearance and lifestyle. The
descriptions of the dinosaurs
are supported by illustrations
that bring these long-extinct
animals vividly to life.

Captions and labels discuss
important features of the
anatomy of each dinosaur.

Like all hadrosaurs, Maiasaura
had a horny, toothless beak at
the front of its mouth.

Ornithopoda

MAIASAURA
Some paleontologists believe that *Maiasaura*
were strongly social animals that lived
in the late Cretaceous period in
herds of many thousands.

Discovery The first fossils ever
found of *Maiasaura* were a huge
nesting colony, about 75 million
years old. It was discovered in the
badlands of Montana in 1978 by
John Horner and Robert Makela.
This colony contained eggs (many
still intact), babies and adults; even
the way the eggs were arranged
could be seen. This seeming
demonstration of parental care
inspired the name of this dinosaur.

Characteristics The proximity
of the nests suggests that females
nested in large groups. Careful
study of the site led to some
interesting insights into the

nurturing habits of *Maiasaura*.
Many of these babies were
clearly too large to be newly
hatched but were evidently still
living in the nest. Like the leg
bones of some species of modern
birds, the bones in the legs of the
baby *Maiasaura* were not fully
formed. Despite this, their teeth
showed signs of wear. The logical
conclusion was that the babies
were being fed in the nest.

280

Main text gives information
about the discovery of each
dinosaur and describes its
characteristics.

TRIASSIC (245–208 mya)   JURASSIC (208–145 my

A timeline covers the three
periods of the Mesozoic era
during which the dinosaurs
evolved and died out.

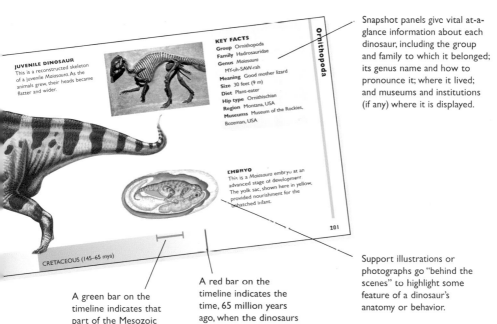

JUVENILE DINOSAUR
This is a reconstructed skeleton of a juvenile *Maiasaura*. As the animals grew, their heads became flatter and wider.

KEY FACTS
Group Ornithopoda
Family Hadrosauridae
Genus *Maiasaura*
    MY-uh-SAW-rah
Meaning Good mother lizard
Size 30 feet (9 m)
Diet Plant-eater
Hip type Ornithischian
Region Montana, USA
Museums Museum of the Rockies, Bozeman, USA

Ornithopoda

Snapshot panels give vital at-a-glance information about each dinosaur, including the group and family to which it belonged; its genus name and how to pronounce it; where it lived; and museums and institutions (if any) where it is displayed.

EMBRYO
This is a *Maiasaura* embryo at an advanced stage of development. The yolk sac, shown here in yellow, provided nourishment for the unhatched infant.

201

Support illustrations or photographs go "behind the scenes" to highlight some feature of a dinosaur's anatomy or behavior.

CRETACEOUS (145–65 mya)

A green bar on the timeline indicates that part of the Mesozoic era in which each dinosaur lived.

A red bar on the timeline indicates the time, 65 million years ago, when the dinosaurs became extinct.

EORAPTOR

Eoraptor was almost certainly a bipedal predator and a very primitive relative of the theropods, one of the earliest groups of dinosaurs. It may have walked on all fours from time to time, but it ran mainly on its hindlimbs. It was probably a very active, fast-moving hunter that preyed on a range of lizard-sized animals.

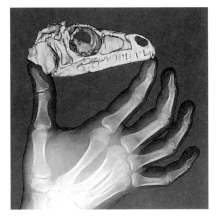

TINY SKULL
This X-ray photograph shows Eoraptor's skull being held by the hand of the paleontologist Paul Sereno whose team discovered this dinosaur in north-western Argentina.

Discovery In 1993, Paul Sereno, Fernando Novas and some colleagues discovered Eoraptor in the Ischigualasto Basin in Argentina. A member of the team was about to discard a piece of rock when he noticed some teeth in it. Closer inspection showed that the rock contained a complete skull. A further search soon unearthed a complete skeleton of perhaps the most primitive of all known dinosaurs.

Characteristics Like other theropods, Eoraptor had thin-walled, hollow bones in its arms and legs, and stood on feet dominated by the three middle toes. Eoraptor had five fingers on each hand, but the fifth finger was very small. We know from Eoraptor's serrated teeth that it was a meat-eater.

H
TRIASSIC (245–208 mya)   JURASSIC (208–145 mya)

Though it was an efficient hunter, Eoraptor did not have a flexible jaw. It relied on its hands in order to trap struggling prey.

The size of Eoraptor's hands suggests that it could handle prey that was almost as large as itself.

Group Saurischia

Family Theropoda

Genus *Eoraptor*
EE-oh-RAP-tuh

Meaning Dawn thief

Size 3 feet 3 inches (1 m)

Diet Meat-eater

Hip type Saurischian

Region North-western Argentina

Museums Not on display

Eoraptor's relatively long tail helped to balance the animal's body as it moved swiftly in pursuit of prey.

CRETACEOUS (145–65 mya)

161

HERRERASAURUS

Herrerasaurus was a very primitive theropod. It was probably a swift-moving, bipedal predator, which, since it was about twice the size of *Eoraptor*, may well have included it in its prey.

Discovery In 1963, Victorino Herrera, an Argentinian goat farmer, was the first person to find a skeleton of *Herrerasaurus*. He came across it in the Ischigualasto Basin in north-western Argentina. In 1988, a team of paleontologists led by Paul Sereno and Fernando Novas discovered a more complete specimen of this dinosaur that finally allowed *Herrerasaurus* to be properly described.

Characteristics *Herrerasaurus* had relatively short forelimbs, with hands that had sickle-shaped claws and an opposable thumb. These hands were well adapted for attacking and grabbing prey. They were similar to those of later theropods except that, like those of *Eoraptor*, they had five fingers. Slightly more advanced theropods lost the fifth finger and in even later theropods the fourth finger disappeared as well.

BUILT FOR SURVIVAL
Bipedal hunters such as *Herrerasaurus* typically had long, slender back limbs and relatively short forelimbs. Both of this dinosaur's jaws had a joint that allowed the animal to open its mouth widely while it fed.

H

TRIASSIC (245–208 mya)   JURASSIC (208–145 mya)

KEY FACTS
Group Theropoda
Family Herrerasauridae
Genus *Herrerasaurus*
huh-RARE-uh-SAW-rus
Meaning Herrera's lizard
Size 6 feet 6 inches (2 m)
Diet Meat-eater
Hip type Saurischian
Region North-western Argentina
Museums Instituto Miguel Lillo,
Tucumán, Argentina; Field Museum,
Chicago, USA

Like other theropods, Herrerasaurus *had hollow, thin-walled bones.*

CRETACEOUS (145–65 mya)

COELOPHYSIS

Coelophysis is one of the most primitive of known theropods. Some of the smallest specimens of *Coelophysis* were found inside the rib cages of larger animals, indicating that this dinosaur may have eaten its own.

VARIED DIET
Coelophysis selected its prey from a wide range of flying insects as well as frogs, mammal-like reptiles and even early mammals.

Coelophysis *had a long, flexible neck and a mouth that opened wide to catch prey.*

H

TRIASSIC (245–208 mya)   JURASSIC (208–145 mya)

Discovery When Edward Drinker Cope first described this dinosaur in 1881, he based his description on a few fragments from Triassic sediments in New Mexico. Almost 70 years later, in 1947, a team of paleontologists made a spectacular discovery of more than 100 skeletons of varying sizes at Ghost Ranch in northern New Mexico. As a result of this find, *Coelophysis* is now one of the best known of all dinosaurs.

Characteristics *Coelophysis* was relatively small. Indeed, some of the skeletons of fully grown adults measured only 5 feet (1.5 m) long—only half the length of the longest known specimens. *Coelophysis* had four fingers on each hand, but the fourth finger was extremely small, and may have been invisible in living animals.

KEY FACTS
Group Theropoda
Family Coelophysidae
Genus *Coelophysis*
   SEE-loh-FIE-sis
Meaning Hollow form
Size 10 feet (3 m)
Diet Meat-eater
Hip type Saurischian
Region North America
Museums American Museum of Natural History, New York, USA; Carnegie Museum, Pittsburgh, USA; Smithsonian Institution, Washington DC, USA; Denver Museum of Natural History, Colorado, USA; Museum of Northern Arizona, Flagstaff, USA

PLATEOSAURUS

Plateosaurus, one of the first of the large dinosaurs, roamed in herds around the northern part of Laurasia during the late Triassic.

A ridge on the lower jaw anchored powerful muscles that produced a very effective bite.

Discovery Many skeletons of *Plateosaurus* have been found in the south of Germany, as well as in France and Switzerland. A mass of skeletons in Germany near the town of Trossingen seems to have resulted from a flash flood that killed a whole herd of *Plateosaurus*. This find was particularly important because it allowed scientists to reconstruct just what a herd of these dinosaurs looked like.

Characteristics *Plateosaurus*, like other prosauropods, had hind legs that were stronger than the front ones and that allowed this dinosaur to rise up to strip leaves from the higher branches of trees.

It probably also reared up when threatened with attack. It had a very large claw on each thumb that would have been an effective defensive weapon. Small patches of bone around the mouth supported cheek pouches that could have held a mouthful of leaves while the front teeth shredded leaves from branches. The cheeks also helped prevent food from falling to the ground while the animal chewed.

TRIASSIC (245–208 mya)   JURASSIC (208–145 mya)

TEETH

Plateosaurus had jaws full of small, pointy teeth of uniform size and shape.

KEY FACTS

Group Sauropodomorpha
Family Plateosauridae
Genus *Plateosaurus*
  PLAY-tee-oh-SAW-rus
Meaning Flat lizard
Size 26 feet (8 m)
Diet Plant-eater
Hip type Saurischian
Region Western Europe
Museums American Museum of Natural History, New York, USA; Senckenberg Nature Museum, Frankfurt, Germany; State Museum of Natural History, Stuttgart, Germany

BALANCING ACT

Plateosaurus's long tail helped to counterbalance the animal's long, thick neck. The hind legs were strong enough to take the animal's weight when it reared up to reach food.

CRETACEOUS (145–65 mya)

RIOJASAURUS

Riojasaurus was a heavily built animal with a long, flexible neck that may have evolved as a response to the dwindling supplies of plant food at ground level as the world dried out at the end of the Triassic.

This bulky animal was probably not capable of rearing up on its back legs. It relied on its long neck to reach high-growing plants.

TRIASSIC (245–208 mya)   JURASSIC (208–145 mya)

Discovery *Riojasaurus*, along with other members of the Sauropodomorpha group, have been found as far afield as South America, South Africa and England.

Characteristics *Riojasaurus* had four robust legs and a bulky body, but its front legs were particularly short. As a result, its head came close to the ground, allowing the dinosaur to graze on low-growing plants. It could also reach up into tree branches and feed on leaves and other foliage. *Riojasaurus's* long neck compensated for its inability to stand up on its hindlimbs. Because sharp, pointed teeth were sometimes found with remains of *Riojasaurus*, some scientists concluded that it was a meat-eater. But we now think that these teeth belonged to predators that fed on newly dead carcasses of *Riojasaurus*.

KEY FACTS

Group Sauropodomorpha

Family Melanorosauridae

Genus *Riojasaurus*
   ree-OH-juh-SAW-rus

Meaning La Rioja lizard

Size 33 feet (10 m)

Diet Plant-eater

Hip type Saurischian

Region La Rioja, Argentina

Museums San Miguel de Tucumán Museum, Argentina

THE BARE BONES
Riojasaurus was one of the first long-necked dinosaurs with hollow bones in its neck. The saurischian hip arrangement is clearly visible in this reconstructed skeleton of *Riojasaurus*.

CRETACEOUS (145–65 mya)

DILOPHOSAURUS

Dilophosaurus, a close relative of *Coelophysis*, was one of the earliest of the large theropods. It was a meat-eater, but probably used its clawed hands and feet rather than its teeth to kill its victims.

Discovery *Dilophosaurus* fossils were first discovered in 1942, in early Jurassic sediments in Arizona, USA. More recently, remains of this dinosaur have been found in China.

Characteristics *Dilophosaurus*, like *Coelophysis*, had four fingers on each hand. The fourth finger, however, was very small and probably had no function. A pair of paper-thin crests ran along the top of *Dilophosaurus's* snout, projecting behind the eyes. Close relatives of *Dilophosaurus*, including *Syntarsis*, had similar, but smaller and less extensive, crests. Scientists cannot be certain how these dinosaurs used these crests, but they may well have served as a signaling device to distinguish one species from another. They may, on the other hand, have been a way of telling the sexes apart. Paleontologists think that *Dilophosaurus*, a meat-eater, probably used its hands and feet to subdue its prey, and then fed on their carcasses. It may also have scavenged animals killed by other predators.

CRESTED SKULL
Dilophosaurus gets its name from the two crests that ran along the top of its snout and head. These crests had shallow pits and holes that may have served as air sacs.

TRIASSIC (245–208 mya) JURASSIC (208–145 mya)

FEEDING TIME

Despite its long, sharp, pointed teeth, *Dilophosaurus*'s jaws were not strong enough for it to feed on live prey.

KEY FACTS

Group Theropoda

Family Coelophysidae

Genus *Dilophosaurus*
die-LOH-foh-SAW-rus

Meaning Two-crested lizard

Size 20 feet (6 m)

Diet Meat-eater

Hip type Saurischian

Region Arizona, USA; China

Museums Museum of Paleontology, University of California, Berkeley, USA; Royal Tyrrell Museum, Alberta, Canada

CRETACEOUS (145–65 mya)

CRYOLOPHOSAURUS

Cryolophosaurus is a relatively large theropod that is known from much of the skull and from a partial skeleton. It is particularly significant because it is the only relatively well-preserved theropod that has been found from the eastern part of Gondwana, in what is now known as Antarctica.

Discovery In 1990, the geologist David Elliott found remains of the carnivorous *Cryolophosaurus* high up near the summit of Mount Kirkpatrick in the central Transantarctic Mountains—what would have been, in the early Jurassic period, the eastern side of the great southern continent of Gondwana. Interestingly, the teeth of two other kinds of theropods that were found in the sediment enclosing the remains suggest that the dead *Cryolophosaurus* had been gnawed by scavengers.

Cryolophosaurus *had serrated, dagger-like teeth.*

Characteristics The distinctive features of *Cryolophosaurus* were the unusual backward-sweeping crests of bone that protruded on the top of the skull above the eyes. Small horns were situated next to these crests, which may have been used during courtship displays or as a way of signaling to other members of the species.

TRIASSIC (245–208 mya)   JURASSIC (208–145 mya)

DISTINCTIVE FORMATION

The crests on *Cryolophosaurus* were formed by the lacrimal bone of the skull. This bone extended along the entire width of the head from between the eyes.

KEY FACTS

Group Theropoda
Family Teranurae (family indeterminate)
Genus *Cryolophosaurus*
    KRY-oh-loh-foh-SAW-rus
Meaning Frozen-crested lizard
Size 24 feet (7.5 m)
Diet Meat-eater
Hip type Saurischian
Region Central eastern Antarctica
Museums Not on display

ANTARCTIC DISCOVERY

A side-on view of the incomplete, but reasonably well-preserved, skull of *Cryolophosaurus* that was discovered by David Elliott in 1990 in Antarctica.

CRETACEOUS (145–65 mya)

ANCHISAURUS

Anchisaurus lived in the area that is now New England at a time when the Atlantic Ocean was just beginning to form. The warm, wet climate was favorable to the growth of huge fern forests that afforded the dinosaurs protection from predators and a supply of food.

Anchisaurus's *tail and neck were relatively long compared with the necks and tails of other prosauropods.*

The curved, sharp claws on Anchisaurus's *hands were an important means of defense.*

TRIASSIC (245–208 mya)   JURASSIC (208–145 mya)

Discovery *Anchisaurus* was the
first dinosaur to be discovered in
America, but it was more than
75 years before it was correctly
identified. The small skeleton that
was discovered in 1818 in a
Connecticut sandstone quarry was,
until 1885, thought to be the
remains of a human. *Anchisaurus*
was one of the many dinosaurs
that were first described by the
American paleontologist Othniel
Charles Marsh.

Characteristics By prosauropod
standards, *Anchisaurus* was very
small, and had a particularly small
head. In overall size, however, its
body was longer than those of
other prosauropods. This dinosaur
could rear up on its back legs
when necessary, although it moved
mainly on all fours. It had rounded
teeth suited to grinding up plants.

FOOTPRINTS
Anchisaurus has
left its footprints
in sandstone
deposits in
Connecticut, USA.

PROOF
These footprints provide some
evidence that *Anchisaurus* could
sometimes walk on only two legs.

KEY FACTS
Group Sauropodomorpha
Family Anchisauridae
Genus *Anchisaurus*
    an-kee-SAW-rus
Meaning Near lizard
Size 8 feet (2.4 m)
Diet Plant-eater
Hip type Saurischian
Region Connecticut,
Massachusetts, USA
Museums South African Museum,
Cape Town, South Africa

MASSOSPONDYLUS

The earliest specimens of *Massospondylus* were
from southern Africa, but later finds were made
in Arizona in the United States. This distribution
was possible in the early Jurassic, when
the continents were still
joined together.

THUMB CLAW
Massospondylus's huge
thumb claw would have been
a formidable defensive weapon.
The thumb claws that were a
prominent feature of many
prosauropods were particularly
well developed in this dinosaur.

TRIASSIC (245–208 mya)   JURASSIC (208–145 mya)

BODY SIZE

Without its long tail and neck, *Massospondylus* would have been only about the size of a large dog.

Massospondylus's mouth contained a variety of tooth types.

Discovery *Massospondylus* was first described by the English anatomist and paleontologist Sir Richard Owen in 1854. He based his description—and named the dinosaur—on the evidence of several large vertebrae.

Characteristics *Massospondylus* was a medium-sized, lightly built prosauropod with much of its length being accounted for by its long neck and tail. It had a particularly small head in which the upper jaw jutted out beyond the bottom one. The variety of tooth types in its mouth has led some researchers to conclude that *Massospondylus* was a carnivore that used its sharper front teeth to rip flesh from prey and its flatter back teeth to chew up this flesh. It has also been suggested that *Massospondylus* could have used its sickle-like thumb claws for predatory purposes. However, most paleontologists now believe that *Massospondylus* was more likely a plant-eater. The fact that grinding stones have been found in its stomach lends strong support to this view.

KEY FACTS

Group Sauropodomorpha
Family Plateosauridae
Genus *Massospondylus*
   MASS-oh-SPON-die-lus
Meaning Massive vertebra
Size 16 feet 6 inches (5 m)
Diet Generally thought to be a plant-eater
Hip type Saurischian
Region Arizona, USA; South Africa; Zimbabwe; Lesotho
Museums South African Museum, Cape Town, South Africa; National Museum of Zimbabwe, Harare, Zimbabwe

CRETACEOUS (145–65 mya)

SCUTELLOSAURUS

Scutellosaurus is one of the earliest of the thyreophorans, or armored dinosaurs—a group that would later include such giants as *Stegosaurus* and *Ankylosaurus*.

Discovery *Scutellosaurus* fossils are found in the United States in the Kayenta Formation of Arizona.

Characteristics *Scutellosaurus* was small, with light armor plating along its back and tail that would have provided some protection from attacks by such predators as *Dilophosaurus*. Some of the small bony "shields" that were embedded in the skin were flat, while others were pitched, like little roofs. The largest shields formed two rows that ran along the middle of the animal's back. Being reasonably fleet of foot as well as armored, *Scutellosaurus* could also escape attackers by weaving through tangled undergrowth. The teeth of *Scutellosaurus* were leaf-shaped and had serrated edges. They were ideally suited to snipping off leaves, but the lack of wear on the teeth indicates that this dinosaur did not chew its food before swallowing it.

SHIELDED SKIN
The bony "shields" on the back of *Scutellosaurus* were varied in size and shape.

TRIASSIC (245–208 mya) | JURASSIC (208–145 mya)

TOP HEAVY

The weight and length of *Scutellosaurus*'s body probably caused this animal to go down on all fours when feeding.

KEY FACTS

Group Thyreophora
Family Scutellosauridae
Genus *Scutellosaurus*
  skoo-TELL-oh-SAW-rus
Meaning Small-shield lizard
Size 4 feet 4 inches (1.3 m)
Diet Plant-eater
Hip type Saurischian
Region Arizona, USA
Museums Museum of Northern
Arizona, Flagstaff, Arizona, USA

Scutellosaurus's *hands were capable of grasping ferns and other foliage, which formed this dinosaur's staple diet.*

CRETACEOUS (145–65 mya)

HETERODONTOSAURUS

Heterodontosaurus was the earliest of the ornithopod dinosaurs. It was small and fast-moving and lived on a diet of plants. Many of the features that would be important to the success of the ornithopods—grinding teeth, fleshy cheeks, the ability to run on back legs—can be seen in ancestral form in this dinosaur.

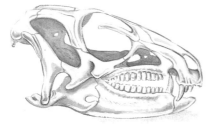

GRASPING HANDS
Heterodontosaurus had relatively long front legs and a "thumb" that enabled it to grasp vegetation.

TUSKS
The two pairs of tusks in *Heterodontosaurus*'s mouth were similar to the canines of a carnivore.

TRIASSIC (245–208 mya)

H
JURASSIC (208–145 mya)

Heterodontosaurus *could run swiftly on its powerful back legs.*

Discovery *Heterodontosaurus* lived in Southern Africa in the early Jurassic period.

Characteristics This dinosaur gets its name from the different types of teeth that lined its jaws. At the front of the mouth were small chopping teeth, while at the back were larger, fatter and more thickly enameled teeth. The back teeth were suitable for grinding plant matter. With these two types of teeth, *Heterodontosaurus* was able to eat plant matter more efficiently than any herbivore that had lived up to that time. *Heterodontosaurus* also had fleshy cheeks that helped it to keep extra food in its mouth while it was chewing. Between the front and back teeth, *Heterodontosaurus* had two pairs of large tusks. These may have enabled it to eat meat as well

as plants, but it seems more likely it used these for digging up roots or for mating displays. We do not know if the tusks were present in only one or in both sexes. This dinosaur had relatively long front legs, and while it may have stood on all fours while grazing on ground plants, if it needed to move quickly, it probably would have run on only its strong back legs.

KEY FACTS
Group Ornithopoda
Family Heterodontosauridae
Genus *Heterodontosaurus*
    HET-uh-roh-DONT-oh-SAW-rus
Meaning Different-toothed lizard
Size 4 feet (1.2 m)
Diet Plant-eater
Hip type Ornithischian
Region South Africa
Museums Smithsonian Institution, Washington DC, USA; South African Museum, Cape Town, South Africa

CRETACEOUS (145–65 mya)

MEGALOSAURUS

Despite its very familar name and its association with the early scientific study of dinosaurs, we know surprisingly little about *Megalosaurus*. Like other theropods, it was probably a bipedal predator with a grasping, three-fingered hand. However, even this is still speculative.

SLOW AND AWKWARD
This bulky creature walked, probably slowly and rather clumsily, on its strong back legs. *Megalosaurus,* like other theropods, probably had grasping three-fingered hands. However, no remnants of the forelimbs have yet been found.

Discovery William Buckland's description of *Megalosaurus* in the early 1820s was the first formal description of a nonavian dinosaur. It was based on a collection of fossil fragments—including parts of a leg, a shoulder, a hip and a jaw—that gave only scant clues to the appearance of the living animal.

Characteristics The available, and still very limited, evidence suggests that this dinosaur was a massive animal. It probably grew 30 feet (9 m) long, stood up to 10 feet (3 m) high, and weighed about 1 ton (1.02 tonnes). It had powerful, hinged jaws and its curved, serrated teeth indicate that it was a strong predator that probably fed on a wide variety of animals, including large sauropods. Just how *Megalosaurus* relates to dinosaurs that evolved later is something of a mystery. It seems that *Megalosaurus* belongs outside the groups that include the allosaurids and the coelurosaurs and is closer to the spinosaurids, although this has not been proved.

TRIASSIC (245–208 mya)   JURASSIC (208–145 mya)

KEY FACTS

Group Theropoda
Family Megalosauridae
Genus *Megalosaurus*
  MEG-uh-loh-SAW-rus
Meaning Great lizard
Size 30 feet (9 m)
Diet Meat-eater
Hip type Saurischian
Region England
Museums Natural History Museum,
London, UK

SAW EDGES
The teeth of *Megalosaurus*
were sharply serrated.

CRETACEOUS (145–65 mya)

CERATOSAURUS

Until recently, paleontologists grouped all large theropod dinosaurs, including *Ceratosaurus*, under the heading "carnosaurs." Scientists now think that this was incorrect. *Ceratosaurus* was probably more closely related to the smaller-bodied coelophysoids and to the Abelisauridae—a group that lived throughout the Southern Hemisphere during the Cretaceous period.

Discovery *Ceratosaurus* is known mainly from the late Jurassic Morrison Formation of the western United States.

Characteristics *Ceratosaurus* has a blunt horn at the end of its snout. It is the best known of several theropods—known as "ceratosaurs"—that had such a snout. *Ceratosaurus* also had two other short, thin horns, one over each eye. We cannot be certain what function these horns served. They may have been used as social signaling devices. They may also have served to distinguish the sexes. As only a few specimens of this dinosaur have been found, we do not know if the sexes had differently shaped horns—or even if both sexes had horns. The horns do not seem large enough to have been used in defense.

TRIASSIC (245–208 mya)   JURASSIC (208–145 mya)

BUILT FOR DEFENSE

Ceratosaurus's horns may have provided protection for the eyes. *Ceratosaurus* had very solid hindlimbs and relatively small forelimbs. Its sharp claws were effective weapons of attack.

KEY FACTS

Group Theropoda
Family Ceratosauridae
Genus *Ceratosaurus*
  seh-RAT-oh-SAW-rus
Meaning Horned lizard
Size 20 feet (6 m)
Diet Meat-eater
Hip type Saurischian
Region North America
Museums American Museum of Natural History, New York, USA; Dinosaur National Monument, Jensen, Utah, USA; Smithsonian Institution, Washington DC, USA

TEETH AND JAWS

Ceratosaurus had sharp, curved teeth and strong jaw muscles that were typical of many theropod dinosaurs.

ALLOSAURUS

Allosaurus belonged to the allosaurids, a group which peaked in the late Jurassic and early Cretaceous and was found in most parts of the world. By the late Cretaceous, their place as formidable hunters had been taken by other large predators such as the tyrannosaurids and abelisaurids.

HUGE, BUT FLEXIBLE
Allosaurus's neck was slender, but very strong and flexible. The hindlimbs of *Allosaurus* were massive, but were proportioned for swift movement.

Discovery The Morrison Formation of the western United States has yielded abundant remains of *Allosaurus*.

Characteristics In many ways *Allosaurus* was a classic example of a large theropod. It had a deep, but light, skull, and jaws with flattened, serrated teeth. The jaws could bend outward in the middle, thus enlarging the mouth and making it possible for this dinosaur to swallow large pieces of flesh whole. The dinosaur's forelimbs were heavily muscled and ended in powerful grasping hands with enormous claws. *Allosaurus* stood on only the middle three of its five toes. This formidable predator was probably a major threat to any ornithopods, stegosaurs or sauropods that lived near it. An earlier name for *Allosaurus*—*Antrodemus*, or "nightmare dragon"—reflects its dominance as a predator in the late Jurassic period.

TRIASSIC (245–208 mya)   JURASSIC (208–145 mya)

HUGE SKULL
The skull of *Allosaurus* could be up to 3 feet (1 m) long.

KEY FACTS
Group Theropoda
Family Allosauridae
Genus *Allosaurus*
 AL-oh-SAW-rus
Meaning Other lizard
Size 39 feet (12 m)
Diet Meat-eater
Hip type Saurischian
Region Western United States
Museums American Museum of Natural History, New York, USA; Dinosaur National Monument, Jensen, Utah, USA; Smithsonian Institution, Washington DC, USA; Los Angeles County Museum, USA; Denver Museum of Natural History, USA

DEADLY BATTLE
An *Allosaurus* (right) and a *Camptosaurus* do battle in this reconstructed scene from 140 million years ago.

ORNITHOLESTES

In 1903, three years after the discovery of this small theropod, Henry Fairfield Osborn described and named the dinosaur. He called it *Ornitholestes* because he believed that, with its swift gait and grasping hands, it would have been good at catching birds in flight. Osborn may have been right, but there is no clear evidence that he was.

SWIFT PREDATOR
Whether hunting or being hunted, with its long, graceful legs, *Ornitholestes* was very fleet of foot.

Discovery In 1900 a group of scientists from the American Museum of Natural History found the first, and so far the only, remains of *Ornitholestes* in the famous Jurassic dinosaur beds at Bone Cabin Quarry in Wyoming in the western United States. The find consisted of an almost complete skeleton and a complete, but compressed, skull.

Characteristics Some researchers have speculated that *Ornitholestes* had a thin horn at the tip of its snout, right above the nose. No horn can be detected on the single existing specimen, but as the tip of the snout is considerably damaged, it is not possible to tell whether or not there was a horn there.

TRIASSIC (245–208 mya)   JURASSIC (208–145 mya)

HORNED SNOUT

This reconstruction of *Ornitholestes*'s skull shows a horn on the tip of the snout.

KEY FACTS

Group Theropoda

Family Coeluridae

Genus *Ornitholestes*
  ORN-ith-oh-LESS-tees

Meaning Bird robber

Size 6 feet 6 inches (2 m)

Diet Meat-eater

Hip type Saurischian

Region North America

Museums American Museum of Natural History, New York, USA

SMALL PREY

Ornitholestes was an agile hunter that preyed upon a variety of small animals. This one is feasting on a salamander.

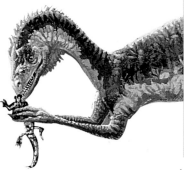

CRETACEOUS (145–65 mya)

COMPSOGNATHUS

Compsognathus was one of the smallest known nonavian dinosaurs. Its name refers to the delicacy of its jaw, but its fossils suggest that it was a delicate animal overall.

HANDS AND FEET
While it is clear that this small dinosaur had three toes on each foot, some scientists believe that it had only two fingers on each hand.

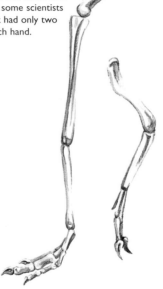

Discovery There are two known fossils of *Compsognathus*. The first, found in 1859, was from the late Jurassic lithographic limestone of southern Germany. It lay on a slab of stone, its legs nearly perfectly preserved and its last meal, a lizard, in its ribcage. The second skeleton was found near Canjuers, in France.

Characteristics *Compsognathus* has long played a central role in studies of bird origins. Because it was found in the same late Jurassic deposits as *Archaeopteryx*, and was about the same size, it provides an easy comparison between a primitive bird and a primitive coelurosaur. In the 19th century, similarities between these two fossils were often cited as evidence of the bird–dinosaur link. It is possible, but not proven, that this little dinosaur may well have had short, fibrous, featherlike structures on its body, although there is no direct evidence of these in the known specimens. It is probable that *Compsognathus* confined itself to catching small victims and that it used its clawed fingers and toothy jaws to do so.

TRIASSIC (245–208 mya)   JURASSIC (208–145 mya)

The long, clawed fingers on the hands were well adapted to grasping small prey.

KEY FACTS

Group Theropoda
Family Compsognathidae
Genus *Compsognathus*
KOMP-sog-NAY-thus
Meaning Delicate jaw
Size 3 feet (1 m)
Diet Meat-eater
Hip type Saurischian
Region South-western Germany; France
Museums Bavarian State Museum of Paleontology, Munich, Germany

SMALL AND DELICATE

Compsognathus stood no taller than a present-day chicken. The tail made up about half this dinosaur's total length.

CRETACEOUS (145–65 mya)

191

ARCHAEOPTERYX

Perhaps the most famous fossil of all is that of *Archaeopteryx*, a tiny feathered dinosaur that is also generally considered to be the earliest known bird.

BIRDLIKE FEATHERS
Archaeopteryx's feathers were arranged in a similar pattern to those of a living bird.

Discovery The first skeleton of *Archaeopteryx* was found in 1861 and since then, six more have come to light. All seven are from the late Jurassic lithographic limestones of Solnhofen, in southern Germany. Remarkably, five of the skeletons are preserved with impressions of the delicate feathers that this dinosaur had in real life. Normally, feathers would not be strong enough to withstand the rigors of fossilization. *Archaeopteryx* displays a clear mix of characters from two linked groups—birds and dinosaurs. It is a classic and rare example of an organism on an evolutionary pathway between the two.

Characteristics *Archaeopteryx* was a small birdlike dinosaur, about the same size as a present-day crow. Its skeleton was in a number of ways very similar to that of some theropod dinosaurs in that it had four toes on each foot, with the first toe in a reverse position to the other three; three fingers on each hand; a long, straight bony tail; teeth; curved claws on the hands and feet; and a large crest on the upper arm bone.

TRIASSIC (245–208 mya)   JURASSIC (208–145 mya)

KEY FACTS

Group Theropoda
Family Aves
Genus *Archaeopteryx*
   AH-kee-OP-tuh-rix
Meaning Ancient feather
Size 2 feet (60 cm)
Diet Meat-eater
Hip type Saurischian
Region Bavaria, Germany
Museums Humboldt Museum,
Berlin, Germany; Natural History
Museum, London, UK

CRETACEOUS (145–65 mya)

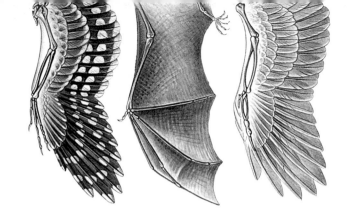

BATS, BIRDS AND DINOSAURS
These illustrations show the strong similarity between the wing structure of *Archaeopteryx* and that of birds, and the way they differ from that of a bat. The wing of a bat (center) is made of skin and supported by all five fingers. An *Archaeopteryx* wing (far left) was made of feathers that had a shape and arrangement similar to those of a modern pigeon (left).

Feathers *Archaeopteryx*'s most strikingly birdlike feature was its feathers. In both their shape and the pattern in which they were arranged, they resembled the flight feathers of birds capable of powered flight. We can probably assume that *Archaeopteryx* was capable of powered flight, but perhaps only for short distances. It probably fed on insects that it found in trees or caught in flight.

As well as the seven complete or partial skeletons of this dinosaur, isolated *Archaeopteryx* feathers have also been found. The excellent state of preservation of the delicate, hollow bones and fine feathers was possible only because the fossils occurred in a very fine-grained limestone known as lithographic limestone. It is so called because it was quarried in Bavaria, Germany, in order to

make lithographic printing plates. It was during these quarrying procedures that the specimens of *Archaeopteryx*, as well as the remains of thousands of other important fossils, were recovered.

DELICATE IMPRESSIONS
The impressions of feathers are clearly visible in this fossil of *Archaeopteryx* which was preserved in lithographic limestone that was quarried in Bavaria, Germany.

CAMARASAURUS

Camarasaurus fossils are more common than those of any other North American sauropod. A number of complete skeletons have been recovered, as well as numerous partial skeletons and isolated bones.

PHYSICAL ADVANTAGES

Camarasaurus's big eyes and large nostrils suggest that it had keen senses of sight and smell to detect predators such as *Allosaurus*. *Camarasaurus* needed a very large stomach in order to digest the tough plant food on which it fed.

TRIASSIC (245–208 mya)　　JURASSIC (208–145 mya)

Discovery In 1877 when the noted American paleontologist Edward Drinker Cope described *Camarasaurus*, he was obviously impressed by the hollow, box-like vertebrae in the neck. This unusual feature made the neck lighter and easier for the animal to carry, and it is this characteristic that gave this dinosaur its name of "chambered lizard."

Characteristics *Camarasaurus* was a stout, compact sauropod, with a relatively short neck and short tail. Huge holes for the eye sockets, nostrils and other skull cavities made the skull as light as possible, but still strong enough to withstand the bite forces from the doglike skull. *Camarasaurus* had strong, stumpy teeth that were much more robust than the peglike teeth of other sauropods.

HOLES IN THE HEAD
Huge nasal openings at the top of the skull may have helped to cool *Camarasaurus*'s brain.

FOSSIL DISPLAY
A *Camarasaurus* fossil in the Devil's Canyon Science and Learning Center, Fruita, Colorado, USA.

KEY FACTS
Group Sauropoda
Family Camarasauridae
Genus *Camarasaurus*
   KAM-uh-ruh-SAW-rus
Meaning Chambered lizard
Size 59 feet (18 m)
Diet Plant-eater
Hip type Saurischian
Region Colorado, Utah, Wyoming, USA; Portugal
Museums Natural History Museum, London, UK; Carnegie Museum of Natural History, Pittsburgh, Pennsylvania, USA; Smithsonian Institution, Washington DC, USA; Peabody Museum, New Haven, Connecticut, USA

DIPLODOCUS

Diplodocus evolved in the late Jurassic period and is one of the longest of all known dinosaurs. It is still the longest dinosaur that we know from a complete skeleton. Most of its length is accounted for by its neck and tail.

DEFENSIVE TOOL
Although *Diplodocus* was not fast enough to outrun a predator, its heavy, strong tail was a powerful defensive weapon.

TRIASSIC (245–208 mya)   JURASSIC (208–145 mya)

Discovery *Diplodocus* fossils have been discovered in Colorado, Utah and Wyoming in the western regions of the United States.

Characteristics *Diplodocus* had a small, horselike head, and its peglike teeth were restricted to the front of its mouth. It used these teeth to strip large quantities of leaves from trees. It then swallowed them whole to await further processing in its huge gut. The last third of its tail was very thin and whiplike, and the vertebrae at the end of the tail were reduced to simple rods. *Diplodocus's* front legs were shorter than its back ones. Its hips were higher than its shoulders, which made its back slope forward.

KEY FACTS
Group Sauropoda
Family Diplodocidae
Genus *Diplodocus*
dip-LOH-doh-kus
Meaning Double beam
Size 90 feet (27 m)
Diet Plant-eater
Hip type Saurischian
Region Wyoming, Colorado, Utah, USA
Museums National History Museum, London, UK; National Museum of Natural History, Paris, France; Carnegie Museum of Natural History, Pittsburgh, Pennsylvania, USA

Diplodocus used its very long neck to reach lush vegetation deep in forests. It had a small head and mouth and needed to spend much time eating in order to nourish its huge body.

LONG AND LIGHT
Diplodocus was longer than *Brachiosaurus*, but weighed only a third as much—partly because its skeleton contained air pockets that reduced its weight but not its strength.

Diplodocus's name—meaning "double beam"—is derived from the bones on the underside of its tail, known as chevrons. In most other dinosaurs, these are simple V-shaped elements, but in this dinosaur they are like side-on Ts, projecting both to the front and the back. Scientists used to think that *Diplodocus*, like other sauropods, was a lumbering beast that dragged its tail along the ground. During the 1980s, however, it dawned on people that although these animals left fossil tracks, there were never any impressions of tails on the ground. It seemed, then, that the tails must have been held high off the ground. How, though, could such a huge animal manage this without enormous effort? The answer was in the tail structure. Examination of *Diplodocus* skeletons revealed that the tendons that ran along the back, from behind the head to the end of the tail, balanced the tail against the weight of the neck and enabled *Diplodocus* to hold its tail out straight behind. This rethinking about posture led to a revision in museum displays around the world. Copies of *Diplodocus* skeletons were taken apart and reconstructed in their new "authentic" pose.

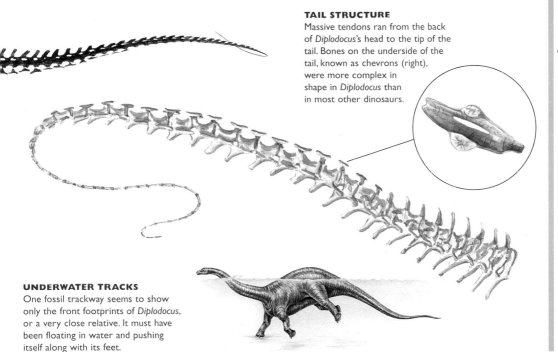

TAIL STRUCTURE
Massive tendons ran from the back of *Diplodocus*'s head to the tip of the tail. Bones on the underside of the tail, known as chevrons (right), were more complex in shape in *Diplodocus* than in most other dinosaurs.

UNDERWATER TRACKS
One fossil trackway seems to show only the front footprints of *Diplodocus*, or a very close relative. It must have been floating in water and pushing itself along with its feet.

BAROSAURUS

Barosaurus was very similar to *Diplodocus*, to which it is closely related. Both were very long animals with relatively compact bodies supporting long necks and tails.

Barosaurus's *long neck and its long, whiplike tail balanced each other like a seesaw.*

TRIASSIC (245–208 mya)   **JURASSIC (208–145 mya)**

PROTECTIVE MOTHER
This dramatic reconstruction in New York's American Museum of Natural History shows an adult female *Barosaurus* defending her infant from an attacking *Allosaurus*.

KEY FACTS
Group Sauropoda
Family Diplodocidae
Genus *Barosaurus*
   BAH-roh-SAW-rus
Meaning Heavy lizard
Size 80 feet (26 m)
Diet Plant-eater
Hip type Saurischian
Region South Dakota, Utah, USA; Tanzania
Museums American Museum of Natural History, New York, USA; Utah Museum of Natural History, Salt Lake City, USA; Dinosaur National Monument, Jensen, Utah, USA

Discovery Despite more than a century of searching and the discovery of five partial skeletons of *Barosaurus*, some of them almost complete, the head and the tip of the tail of this dinosaur have never been found. The only clues we have about the head are a few bones from the skull, which were collected in Tanzania, and comparisons with close relatives such as *Diplodocus*.

Characteristics These bones indicate that *Barosaurus* had a horselike skull with a long snout and teeth restricted to the very front of the mouth. *Barosaurus*'s neck stretched out about 30 feet (9 m) from the shoulders. Like *Diplodocus*, *Barosaurus* had front legs shorter than the hind ones. *Barosaurus*'s neck vertebrae would not have permitted much up-and-down movement, but would have allowed a wide sweep from side to side. It probably fed mainly close to the ground on ferns and cycads.

MAMENCHISAURUS

Although superficially *Mamenchisaurus* looks
similar to North American sauropods such as
Diplodocus and *Apatosaurus*, we now think that it
was part of a group of sauropods unique to Asia.

LONG NECK
Mamenchisaurus's neck was about
six times as long as the neck of
a modern giraffe. The neck ended
in a small head and short snout.

TRIASSIC (245–208 mya)   JURASSIC (208–145 mya)

Discovery *Mamenchisaurus* was described in 1954 by the Chinese scientist Chung Chien Young, who is regarded as the father of Chinese vertebrate paleontology.

Characteristics The neck of *Mamenchisaurus* was longer than the neck of any other animal that we know about. It allowed it to feed comfortably from the tree tops and made up about half the animal's total length. Reaching perhaps 49 feet (15 m) long, this incredible structure was supported by 19 vertebrae—no other dinosaur had as many neck vertebrae. Because these vertebrae were hollow—and in places the bone was as thin as egg shells—the neck was very light. Long bony struts running between the neck vertebrae would have limited its flexibility, and reconstructions of this dinosaur often show it with the neck held out straight as a ramrod. Some of these bony struts would have overlapped three or four vertebrae. Despite the great length of its neck, *Mamenchisaurus's* tail was considerably shorter than those of its close relatives *Barosaurus* and *Diplodocus*. Only a few skull fragments from *Mamenchisaurus* have been found. These suggest that it had a relatively short snout with robust, blunt teeth in the front and along the sides of the mouth. The very heavy teeth give a clue to this animal's diet. These teeth could have dealt with the coarser, harder parts of plants and would have been good for shredding cycads and other fibrous fronds.

KEY FACTS

Group Sauropoda

Family Diplodocidae

Genus *Mamenchisaurus* mah-MEN-kee-SAW-rus

Meaning Mamen Brook lizard

Size 82 feet (25 m)

Diet Plant-eater

Hip type Saurischian

Region Szechuan, Gansu, Xinjiang, China

Museums Beijing Natural History Museum, Beijing, China; Museum Victoria, Melbourne, Australia

APATOSAURUS

Apatosaurus is a less familiar name than *Brontosaurus*, but they are one and the same animal.

SLOPING BODY

As with many other sauropods, *Apatosaurus*'s front legs were shorter than its back ones and, as a result, its body sloped forward.

TRIASSIC (245–208 mya)   JURASSIC (208–145 mya)

WRONG HEAD
Early reconstructions of
Apatosaurus mistakenly showed
it with the skull of *Camarasaurus*
(above). The correct skull is
shown at the far right.

KEY FACTS
Group Sauropoda
Family Diplodocidae
Genus *Apatosaurus*
  uh-PAT-oh-SAW-rus
Meaning Deceptive lizard
Size 69 feet (21 m)
Diet Plant-eater
Hip type Saurischian
Region Colorado, Utah, Wyoming,
Oklahoma, USA; Baja California,
Mexico
Museums American Museum of
Natural History, New York, USA;
Carnegie Museum of Natural History,
Pittsburgh, Pennsylvania, USA;
Dinosaur National Monument, Jensen,
Utah, USA

Discovery *Apatosaurus* fossils have been discovered in the western regions of the United States and Baja California in Mexico. Several gigantic, and relatively complete, skeletons were found and displayed worldwide under the name *Brontosaurus* before it became evident that they were identical to those of *Apatosaurus*, which had been named earlier. After this, the dinosaur became officially known as *Apatosaurus*.

Characteristics It is a puzzle how a head and mouth as small as those of *Apatosaurus* could have gathered enough food to feed its huge body, especially as the teeth could not chew the food—they merely cut off leaves, which were then swallowed whole. It seems that *Apatosaurus* spent long periods stripping vegetation. This food was held in a vatlike foregut where it stewed up, gradually breaking down to release its nutrients.

STEGOSAURUS

One of the most famous dinosaurs of all, *Stegosaurus* is striking, first of all for its great size, but more so for the bizarre plates and spikes that stand up like battlements on each side of its backbone.

DISTINGUISHING FEATURE
The plates that stood up along the back of *Stegosaurus* are its most remarkable feature. The function of these is still a matter of considerable speculation.

TRIASSIC (245–208 mya)　　　JURASSIC (208–145 mya)

Until fairly recently scientists thought that Stegosaurus *dragged its tail along the ground. They now believe that it held its tail high.*

Discovery Othniel Charles Marsh described the first specimen of *Stegosaurus* in 1877. He originally thought that the unusual plates on the back lay flat, forming a kind of roof. In fact, that is how this dinosaur got its inaccurate, but enduring, name. But what function did these plates serve? Perhaps they provided protection from attack. Channels in the plates that contained blood vessels suggest that they may have helped to control body temperature. By turning the plates broadside to the sun, *Stegosaurus* could have warmed its blood; by turning them edge-on to the sun, it could have cooled its blood. They may also have been used for display. Perhaps, when flushed with blood, the plates could change color in order to impress a potential mate or to scare off a predator.

KEY FACTS

Group Stegosauria
Family Stegosauridae
Genus *Stegosaurus*
   STEG-oh-SAW-rus
Meaning Roofed lizard
Size 29 feet 6 inches (9 m)
Diet Plant-eater
Hip type Ornithischian
Region Colorado, Utah, Wyoming, USA
Museums American Museum of Natural History, New York, USA; Dinosaur National Monument, Jensen, Utah, USA; Denver Museum, Colorado, USA; Senckenberg Nature Museum, Frankfurt, Germany

Stegosauria

Characteristics As well as the unusual plates, *Stegosaurus* had spikes at the end of its tail that could reach more than 3 feet (1 m) in length. These would have been a very effective weapon. The heavily built hind legs carried the bulk of *Stegosaurus*'s weight. They were almost twice as long as the front legs. This meant that this dinosaur walked with its head, shoulders and neck close to the ground. *Stegosaurus* had a small head with a long snout. Its teeth were small, and the wear on fossil remains indicates that it ground the upper and lower teeth together to cut and slice food. All the teeth were at the rear of the mouth. At the front it had a horny beak that could cut through plants as effectively as a pair of shears. Recent research suggests that *Stegosaurus* had cheek pouches in which it could hold food that was waiting to be chewed.

PLATED SKELETON
This reproduction of a *Stegosaurus* skeleton shows how the plates were staggered rather than symmetrically paired, as was once thought.

CHANGING PLATES

These diagrams show how the angle and shape of the plates varied along different parts of the animal's back and tail. On the tail, the plates were replaced by matched pairs of outward-pointing sharp spikes.

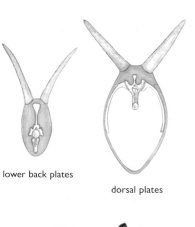

tip of tail spikes

lower back plates

dorsal plates

The long, sharp spikes on a swinging tail spelled danger for would-be predators.

TINY BRAIN

For its size, *Stegosaurus* had the smallest brain of any dinosaur. Its brain was about the size of a walnut.

KENTROSAURUS

Among the most important and best preserved dinosaurs to be recovered from the Tendaguru Hill dinosaur find in Tanzania were hundreds of bones of the armored dinosaur *Kentrosaurus*.

Discovery This dinosaur was named by the German paleontologist Edwin Henning in 1915, during World War I. This illustration is based on a copy of the skeleton that is now on display in Tübingen, but new evidence from China now places the pelvic spike on the shoulder.

Characteristics *Kentrosaurus* had as many as seven pairs of spikes extending from the end of the tail onto the lower back. In front of the spikes were seven pairs of plates extending forward to the neck. *Kentrosaurus* fed close to the ground, using a cropping beak at the front of the mouth and small chomping teeth farther back. Although *Kentrosaurus* is superficially similar to its larger American cousin *Stegosaurus*, it is probably more closely related to the contemporary Chinese stegosaur *Tuojiangosaurus* and the slightly later *Wuerhosaurus*.

BRAIN CASTS
These brain casts have been taken from the two *Kentrosaurus* fossils that have so far been found.

TRIASSIC (245–208 mya)   JURASSIC (208–145 mya)

KEY FACTS
Group Stegosauria
Family Stegosauridae
Genus *Kentrosaurus*
KENT-roh-SAW-rus
Meaning Spiky lizard
Size 16 feet (4.9 m)
Diet Plant-eater
Hip type Ornithischian
Region Tanzania
Museums Natural History Museum,
Humboldt University, Berlin, Germany;
Institute and Museum for Geology
and Paleontology, University of
Tübingen, Germany

PLATES AND SPIKES
Unlike *Stegosaurus*, *Kentrosaurus* had
back plates that were arranged in
symmetrical pairs. About seven pairs
of spikes extended from the end of
the tail to the lower back.

TUOJIANGOSAURUS

Tuojiangosaurus is a stegosaur, a member of the group of armored dinosaurs that includes *Stegosaurus*, *Kentrosaurus* and *Wuerhosaurus*.

Discovery Fossils of two partial skeletons of *Tuojiangosaurus* have been recovered from Szechuan in China, but large parts of its skeleton still remain to be found.

Characteristics An almost complete skull tells us a lot about *Tuojiangosaurus*. Like other stegosaurs, *Tuojiangosaurus* had small teeth at the sides of the mouth, a relatively long, low snout and a tiny brain. Another two, and smaller, stegosaurs—*Chungkingosaurus* and *Chialingosaurus*—lived in China alongside *Tuojiangosaurus* in the late Jurassic. The three may have coexisted by dividing up the plants they ate based on the height at which they fed. It is also possible that the smaller dinosaurs lived in forests, while *Tuojiangosaurus* lived in a more open environment. All three had different-shaped plates, which suggests that they used them for sexual display in attempts to win mates of their own species.

SPIKED TAIL
Tuojiangosaurus's tail was tipped by two stiletto-like spikes. With one swing of its tail, this dinosaur could puncture a predator's belly.

214

TRIASSIC (245–208 mya)   JURASSIC (208–145 mya)

KEY FACTS

Group Stegosauria
Family Stegosauridae
Genus *Tuojiangosaurus*
toh-HWANG-oh-SAW-rus
Meaning Tuo River lizard
Size 23 feet (7 m)
Diet Plant-eater
Hip type Ornithischian
Region Szechuan, China
Museums Zigong Dinosaur
Museum, Szechuan, China;
Shanghai Museum, Shanghai, China;
Beipei Museum, Szechuan, China

BODY TEMPERATURE

Tuojiangosaurus's 17 pairs of bony back plates may have been covered with skin that was rich with blood to help the dinosaur warm up or cool down quickly. *Tuojiangosaurus*'s back plates petered out halfway along the tail.

CRETACEOUS (145–65 mya)

215

IGUANODON

Iguanodon could almost be called a "founding father" of dinosaurs—not in the sense that it is ancestral to other dinosaurs, but in terms of our scientific understanding of dinosaurs.

Discovery *Iguanodon* was widespread in the early Cretaceous. Species have been described from Europe, North America and Mongolia. The first fossils of this dinosaur to be found came from the Wealden rocks of southern England. The very first fossils were only teeth, which resembled the teeth of living iguanas—hence the name. As more bones were found, this dinosaur was reconstructed as a large, lumbering quadrupedal herbivore, and, in what proved to be one of the most famous mistakes in paleontology, a large spike that was found with other parts of the skeleton was placed on the end of the nose. In 1878, workers in a Belgian coal mine discovered a large bone. This led, three years later, to the discovery of 31 complete, and superbly well-preserved, skeletons of *Iguanodon*.

TRIASSIC (245–208 mya)   JURASSIC (208–145 mya)

KEY FACTS
Group Ornithopoda
Family Iguanodontidae
Genus *Iguanodon*
ig-WAN-oh-don
Meaning Iguana tooth
Size 33 feet (10 m)
Diet Plant-eater
Hip type Ornithischian
Region Western USA; Western
Europe; Romania; Mongolia
Museums Royal National Institute
of Natural Sciences, Brussels, Belgium

CRETACEOUS (145–65 mya)

Characteristics The Belgian specimens showed that *Iguanodon* was not, as was previously assumed, a heavy, lumbering quadruped, but was relatively light for its size and could move on its back legs. They also showed that the spike belonged not on the nose, but on the thumb of each hand. *Iguanodon* did spend some time moving around on all fours, and probably ran on its back legs mainly when it needed to move quickly, for example, when it needed to escape from a predator. As in other ornithopods, its spine was supported by large, ossified tendons around the hips.

Iguanodon was an efficient plant-eater. A battery of closely packed cheek teeth was well suited to grinding up tough plant matter—the upper surface of each tooth was broad and ridged. The jaw bones that held the teeth moved upward and outward in the skull as the animal chewed, allowing the grinding surfaces to move against each other, and therefore contributing to the efficiency of the chewing action.

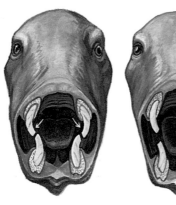

CHEWING ACTION
When an ornithopod dinosaur such as *Iguanodon* closed its mouth to chew its food, the action caused its upper jaw to swing outward (far left). The teeth in the upper jaw and the teeth in the lower jaw then ground against one another. Any food caught in the middle was shredded like a carrot in a grater.

RECONSTRUCTION
This reconstructed *Iguanodon* skeleton is based on an original in the Royal National Institute of Natural Sciences in Belgium.

THUMB SPIKE
Iguanodon used its hand in many ways: for walking, for grasping food and for self-defense. It could also use its spike to injure or kill a predator.

BRACHIOSAURUS

One of the tallest known dinosaurs to walk on all fours, *Brachiosaurus* towered at least 52 feet (16 m) into the forest canopy, where its small head could strip leaves from tree branches. Some finds in the western United States suggest *Brachiosaurus* may have been able to reach much higher. If that is true, it would have been one of the largest of all dinosaurs.

HUGE NOSTRILS
Brachiosaurus had huge nostrils directly above its eye sockets. By pumping blood through the delicate skin inside these nostrils, this dinosaur was able to cool its brain when it became overheated.

Discovery Important specimens of *Brachiosaurus* were recovered by German paleontologists from the rich fossil grounds of Tendaguru in present-day Tanzania. An American specimen collected from Colorado is the largest mounted modern dinosaur skeleton in North America.

Characteristics The sheer size of *Brachiosaurus* would have protected an adult dinosaur from predators, but juveniles would have been vulnerable to attack. It is likely that *Brachiosaurus* formed small herds, in which the larger animals could protect the smaller from the menace of predators. Its long forearms pushed the shoulders high above the level of the hips, producing the characteristic slope of its back. All of its four legs were straight, columnlike pillars.

TRIASSIC (245–208 mya)   JURASSIC (208–145 mya)

UNUSUAL SAUROPOD

Unlike other sauropods, *Brachiosaurus* had front legs that were much longer than its back legs and its body sloped backward. As a result, it was not able to rear up on its back legs.

KEY FACTS

Group Sauropoda
Family Brachiosauridae
Genus *Brachiosaurus*
 BRAK-ee-oh-SAW-rus
Meaning Arm lizard
Period Cretaceous
Size 82 feet (25 m)
Diet Plant-eater
Hip type Saurischian
Region Colorado, Wyoming, Utah, USA; Portugal; Algeria; Tanzania
Museums Humboldt Museum, Berlin, Germany; The Field Museum of Natural History, Chicago, USA

In relation to its body size, Brachiosaurus *had a rather small head. By sauropod standards,* Brachiosaurus *had a relatively short tail.*

SINOSAUROPTERYX

Sinosauropteryx was a small, advanced theropod dinosaur that lived in the early Cretaceous period. Its skeleton indicated that most of its body was covered with impressions of a strange fuzz, a coat of fine filaments more than 1 inch (2.5 cm) long.

BIRDLIKE FEATURES

Sinosauropteryx had sharp curved teeth suitable for tearing the flesh of small mammals. A furlike coat covered much of the upper parts of *Sinosauropteryx*'s body.

TRIASSIC (245–208 mya)   JURASSIC (208–145 mya)

EARLY FEATHERS
A fossil of a juvenile *Sinosauropteryx* shows "protofeathers," an epidermal feature that evolved before true feathers, rising from behind the head and on the neck and back.

Discovery A perfectly preserved skeleton of *Sinosauropteryx* was found in the Liaoning deposits in China and revealed to the world in 1996, causing a sensation in the world of paleontology.

Characteristics Skin impressions found for some dinosaurs reveal that they had scales. But the growing recognition that birds evolved from dinosaurs raised the possibility that some dinosaurs had feathers, or at least some kind of downy body covering that later evolved into the feathers of present-day birds. Then *Sinosauropteryx* was discovered, and much of its back, rump and tail was covered in a fine fuzz that appeared to be made up of thousands of short, single strands. It was less complex than a feather, but was more intricate than simple reptilian scales. The fuzzy coat seemed to form a downy layer that would have been ideal for trapping body heat and keeping the animal warm. This observation lends more weight to the ongoing debate that some dinosaurs were warm-blooded. It is also possible that the fuzz was used as a means of display to attract mates.

KEY FACTS
Group Theropoda
Family Coelurosauridae
Genus *Sinosauropteryx*
SIGH-no-saw-ROP-tuh-rix
Meaning Chinese lizard feather
Size 3 feet (1 m)
Diet Meat-eater
Hip type Saurischian
Region Liaoning, China
Museums Not on display

CARNOTAURUS

This bizarre-looking theropod, distinguished by a pair of sharp, short horns that projected outward above its tiny eye sockets, is known from only a single specimen.

Carnotaurus moved on its two hindlimbs. The forelimbs were so short and minute that they could not have been of much use.

LUMPY SKIN

The skin of *Carnotaurus* was covered with lumps that had a pebbly texture. They did not overlap like the scales on many reptiles.

TRIASSIC (245–208 mya)   JURASSIC (208–145 mya)

Discovery *Carnotaurus* was discovered by the Argentinian paleontologist José Bonaparte in the Patagonia region of Argentina. The skeleton was almost complete, and there were some impressions of skin. The whole specimen was protected by a large concretion—a section of very hard rock. Bonaparte concluded that this dinosaur belonged to a hitherto unknown theropod family—the Abelisauridae. Other abelisaurids were later discovered in India, Argentina and Madagascar. This suggests that these landmasses were connected at some point during the Jurassic or the Cretaceous. No abelisaurids have been found anywhere else.

Characteristics The skin impressions that covered much of *Carnotaurus*'s body and part of the skull, were said to be reptile-like. However, the scales on the skin did not overlap as they do on some reptiles. *Carnotaurus*'s teeth, like those of other abelisaurids, were sharp and serrated. They seemed to splay out from the sides and gave the face a rather triangular look when seen from the front. *Carnotaurus* had hands with four digits at the end of extremely short forelimbs.

KEY FACTS
Group Theropoda
Family Abelisauridae
Genus *Carnotaurus*
KAR-noh-TAW-rus
Meaning Meat bull
Size 16 feet (5 m)
Diet Meat-eater
Hip type Saurischian
Region Argentina
Museums Los Angeles County Museum, USA; Argentine Museum of Natural Sciences, Buenos Aires, Argentina

SHORT FACE
Carnotaurus had a short face, rather like that of a bulldog, with a pair of horns over the eyes.

BARYONYX

Baryonyx and its relatives, the spinosaurids, by virtue of their very enlarged thumb claws, were most unusual theropods that lived in the early Cretaceous period.

Baryonyx gets its name from the huge thumb claw on each of its hands.

GRABBING PREY
Baryonyx's hands were more massive than those of other theropods. They were ideally suited to grasping small prey.

226

TRIASSIC (245–208 mya)   JURASSIC (208–145 mya)

Discovery The first part of *Baryonyx* to be discovered was a huge thumb claw. In 1983, the amateur fossil-hunter William Walker found it in a clay pit in Surrey, England. A group of paleontologists from London's Natural History Museum visited the site and uncovered most of the skeleton of *Baryonyx*.

Characteristics *Baryonyx* had very powerful forelimbs, strong, grasping hands and large thumb claws. Many scientists believe that *Baryonyx* fed mainly on fish, which it grasped in its hands or snapped from the water in its long, slender snout. Its teeth were less flattened than those of most theropods and were very finely serrated. Its teeth and jaws were probably not suited to attacking and bringing down large animals, hence the fish diet.

KEY FACTS
Group Theropoda
Family Spinosauridae
Genus *Baryonyx*
    BARE-ee-ON-icks
Meaning Heavy claw
Size 30 feet (9 m)
Diet Meat-eater
Hip type Saurischian
Region Southern England
Museums Natural History Museum, London, UK

CRETACEOUS (145–65 mya)

SUCHOMIMUS

Suchomimus, one of the largest known spinosaurid dinosaurs, lived in the early Cretaceous period. Several fossils have been found in different sites in Niger, northern Africa.

Discovery *Suchomimus* was discovered in Niger by a party of paleontologists led by Paul Sereno from the University of Chicago, and was first described in 1998.

Characteristics Like *Baryonyx*, *Suchomimus* had pointed, finely serrated teeth. The nature of the teeth, together with its gracile snout, suggest that *Suchomimus* may have been unable to catch large prey and so fed mainly on fish, possibly either picking them up with its muzzle or grasping them with its bladelike claws. Like other spinosaurids, this dinosaur had a low and slender snout.

Suchomimus and other spinosaurids had a secondary palate. The nasal passages stretched all the way to the back of the mouth cavity, as they do in living mammals and crocodiles, and did not open within the mouth, as they do in many living reptiles and most dinosaurs. This was possible because the nasal openings were set back from the tip of the snout. The secondary palate may have strengthened the narrow snout or even allowed *Suchomimus* to keep the tip of the snout submerged while it hunted for fish.

THUMB CLAWS
Like *Baryonyx*, *Suchomimus* had massive forelimbs and a sickle-like claw on each thumb.

228

TRIASSIC (245–208 mya)   JURASSIC (208–145 mya)

Suchomimus's tail was relatively short, but it was flexible and whiplike.

KEY FACTS

Group Theropoda

Family Spinosauridae

Genus *Suchomimus*
SOO-koh-MY-mus

Meaning Crocodile mimic

Size 36 feet (11 m)

Diet Meat-eater

Hip type Saurischian

Region Niger, northern Africa

Museums Children's Museum, Chicago, USA

CROCODILE-LIKE
Suchomimus's very elongated jaws closely resembled those of a modern crocodile.

DEINONYCHUS

Deinonychus was one of the largest of the dromaeosaurids, and was the first to be fully described. After *Deinonychus* was described, the dromaeosaurids became recognized as some of the most chillingly efficient predators that have ever lived.

TAIL LENGTH
Deinonychus's tail accounted for about half of this dinosaur's total length.

Discovery Grant Meyer and Professor John Ostrom of Yale University first found remains of *Deinonychus* in southern Montana in 1964. At the site they unearthed skeletons of four *Deinonychus*, together with a skeleton 20 feet (6 m) long of the ornithopod *Tenontosaurus*.

Characteristics *Deinonychus* was an agile bipedal predator that had a relatively large brain and a long, narrow snout lined with recurved, serrated, bladelike teeth. *Deinonychus* was an intelligent, very well-equipped predator that used the three long-clawed fingers on each of its large hands to snatch small prey or inflict wounds on large animals. It may even have used them as grappling hooks to clamber onto the bodies of larger dinosaurs that it hunted in packs. *Deinonychus*'s tail was stiffened for most of its length by bundles of overlapping bony rods, which were flexible at the base. This stiffening allowed the tail to be controlled by a few large muscles that connected to the hips and the hindlimbs. It helped *Deinonychus* to run faster and more efficiently, and to make rapid lunges or to change direction suddenly while running.

TRIASSIC (245–208 mya)   JURASSIC (208–145 mya)

Deinonychus *had large eyes that were partly forward-facing.*

KEY FACTS

Group Theropoda

Family Dromaeosauridae

Genus *Deinonychus*
die-NON-ee-kus

Meaning Terrible claw

Size 10 feet (3 m)

Diet Meat-eater

Hip type Saurischian

Region Montana, Wyoming, Oklahoma, USA

Museums Peabody Museum of Natural History, New Haven, Connecticut, USA

CRETACEOUS (145–65 mya)

Strength in numbers When John Ostrom first described and named *Deinonychus* in 1969, he suggested that the finding of *Tenontosaurus* together with several *Deinonychus* at the same site indicated a grouping of predators and prey. He put forward the theory that *Tenontosaurus* was *Deinonychus*'s preferred quarry and that here was evidence for pack hunting behavior in *Deinonychus*. Certainly, a single *Deinonychus* would not have been capable of killing a herbivore as large as *Tenontosaurus*, though the death of four *Deinonychus* in the attack could not be considered typical. If, as seems probable, *Deinonychus* did live in packs and hunted larger dinosaurs, it must have been similar to present-day wolves and hyenas. This suggests that *Deinonychus* was not only an acrobatic predator, but that it was part of a caring, cooperative social group. Territories near the migration routes or breeding sites of large herbivores could have supported large packs of 20 or more *Deinonychus*, dominated by a few breeding individuals.

RECONSTRUCTION
This dramatic model of *Deinonychus* vividly emphasizes this dinosaur's predatory features.

PACK HUNTERS

In this painting at the left, two *Deinonychus* fight each other in the foreground, while others have formed a pack to attack a *Tenontosaurus*.

LETHAL CLAWS

Deinonychus's foot was equipped with four sharply clawed toes. The second toe was the largest and was capable of swiveling around through 180 degrees. It was a highly flexible weapon.

MINMI

Minmi was the first armored dinosaur to be found anywhere in the Southern Hemisphere. It is also the best known and most complete dinosaur from Australia.

BROAD AND BONY

Minmi had very broad hips that formed a bony raft across the rump. Bony shields covered much of *Minmi*'s body.

TRIASSIC (245–208 mya)   JURASSIC (208–145 mya)

Discovery *Minmi* was first described from a set of three vertebrae found in southern Queensland during the 1960s. An almost complete skeleton was found in 1990 in Hughenden, in central Queensland.

Characteristics Like other ankylosaurs, *Minmi* had a back covered by rows of bony shields and nubbins. Unlike in most other ankylosaurs, however, this armor extended onto the flanks and belly and even onto the upper parts of all four legs. The tail had two rows of large, bladed spikes occurring in pairs for most of its length. Similar to other ankylosaurs, *Minmi* was a broad but squat animal with four short legs. The head was generally flattened and quite broad at the back, narrowing to a thin snout.

The front of this snout had a horny beak with which this dinosaur snipped off leaves from low vegetation. The leaves were then sliced into small pieces by rows of small teeth along the sides of the mouth.

FOSSIL SKELETON
This skeleton of *Minmi*, found in 1990, is in hard limestone that is slowly being dissolved in weak acid in order to release the bones. This process will take many years.

KEY FACTS
Group Ankylosauria
Family Uncertain
Genus *Minmi*
    MIN-mee
Meaning From Minmi Crossing
Size 8 feet (2.5 m)
Diet Plant-eater
Hip type Ornithischian
Region Queensland, Australia
Museums The Queensland Museum, Brisbane, Australia

CRETACEOUS (145–65 mya)

HYPSILOPHODON

One of the most famous of small dinosaurs, *Hypsilophodon* was also one of the earliest to be studied. It was named after the strong ridges that were visible on its teeth.

FRONT TEETH
Unlike *Dyosaurus*, and most other ornithopods, *Hypsilophodon* still retained some front teeth in the upper jaw.

TRIASSIC (245–208 mya)   JURASSIC (208–145 mya)

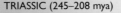

BUILT FOR SPEED
Hypsilophodon's long hind legs were well suited to running at high speed.

Discovery *Hypsilophodon* was discovered in 1849. It was found in the same Wealden rocks in southern England that had yielded *Iguanodon* 20 years earlier. Indeed, at first this animal was thought to have been a juvenile *Iguanodon* until in 1869, Thomas Henry Huxley recognized it as a different dinosaur and named it accordingly.

Characteristics *Hypsilophodon*'s teeth and jaws were well adapted for grinding the tough plant matter on which this animal fed. It had a fleshy cheek, where food could be stored before it was chewed, and a horny beak that cropped food as it entered the mouth. Huxley recognized that this small animal would have been agile and would have moved principally on its hind legs. This surprised many people at a time when most scientists still thought that all dinosaurs were ponderous and moved slowly on all fours. Early reconstructions of *Hypsilophodon*'s foot mistakenly showed it to have a reversed first toe. This led many scientists to believe that it was a tree-dweller. When, finally, the foot was reconstructed correctly, this dinosaur was brought to ground as a fast-running ornithopod.

KEY FACTS
Group Ornithopoda
Family Hypsilophodontidae
Genus *Hypsilophodon*
    HIP-sill-OFF-oh-don
Meaning High-ridged tooth
Size 7 feet (2.2 m)
Diet Plant-eater
Hip type Ornithischian
Region Isle of Wight, England
Museums Natural History Museum, London, UK

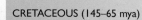

CRETACEOUS (145–65 mya)

QANTASSAURUS

Named for Qantas, the national airline of Australia, *Qantassaurus* belonged to the hypsilophodontids, a group that first appeared in the middle Jurassic, but became very diverse in the early Cretaceous of what is now south-eastern Australia.

Qantassaurus's *tail was about as long as the head and body combined.*

Discovery Since 1978, many isolated or broken bones and teeth of hypsilophodontids have been found near the south coast of Victoria. In 1999, in a tunnel cut into the hard rock at the base of a sea cliff at a place known as Dinosaur Cove, the remains of *Qantassaurus*—the fourth hypsilophodontid dinosaur to be named—were unearthed. From the range of different-sized and different-shaped femora (upper leg bones), it has become clear that various kinds of hypsilophodontids—possibly five or six—coexisted in this habitat.

Characteristics *Qantassaurus* was a bipedal herbivore with a short, deep head and five-fingered hands. It was about the same size as a present-day kangaroo. Unlike a kangaroo, however, it was a runner rather than a hopper—or so we can presume, for other hypsilophodontids that we know from more complete remains certainly ran on two legs.

SPARSE EVIDENCE
The only specimens that paleontologists are convinced belonged to *Qantassaurus* are fossils of the lower jaw and teeth.

TRIASSIC (245–208 mya)   JURASSIC (208–145 mya)

KEY FACTS

Group Ornithopoda
Family Hypsilophodontidae
Genus *Qantassaurus*
  KWON-tuh-SAW-rus
Meaning Qantas lizard
Size 6 feet (2 m)
Diet Plant-eater
Hip type Ornithischian
Region Victoria, Australia
Museums Museum Victoria,
Melbourne, Australia

Qantassaurus *had
long hind legs with
four-toed feet.*

CRETACEOUS (145–65 mya)

ATLASCOPCOSAURUS

Atlascopcosaurus was one of several small hypsilophodontid dinosaurs that lived in what is now south-eastern Australia during the early Cretaceous, a time when the rift between Australia and Antarctica was just beginning to open.

Atlascopcosaurus *used its horny beak to break off tough vegetation in the forest understories.*

TRIASSIC (245–208 mya)   JURASSIC (208–145 mya)

Discovery *Atlascopcosaurus* was named after the company that provided drilling equipment for the Dinosaur Cove digs in Victoria in the late 1980s. Dr. Tom Rich and Dr. Patricia Vickers-Rich who conducted these digs, described this dinosaur in 1989.

Characteristics *Atlascopcosaurus*, like other hypsilophodontids, was an agile bipedal plant-eater. Its upper teeth were similar to those of *Zephyrosaurus*, from Montana, USA, but the primary ridge on each of *Atlascopcosaurus*'s teeth was more strongly developed. *Zephyrosaurus* was also a somewhat smaller animal. *Atlascopcosaurus* used its high-crowned, many-ridged teeth for browsing on the tough ferns and horsetails that formed the understory of forests along the rift valley. The left shin

RICH MINE
This mine, cut into a sea cliff at Dinosaur Cove in south-eastern Victoria, Australia, yielded a number of new dinosaur species.

KEY FACTS
Group Ornithopoda
Family Hypsilophodontidae
Genus *Atlascopcosaurus*
AT-las-KOP-koh-SAW-rus
Meaning Atlas Copco lizard
Size 9 feet (2.7 m)
Diet Plant-eater
Hip type Ornithischian
Region Victoria, Australia
Museums Museum Victoria, Melbourne, Australia

bone of a partial skeleton, thought to be that of *Atlascopcosaurus*, shows evidence that the animal suffered from chronic osteomyelitis for the last few years of its life. The fact that a crippled animal could survive for some years suggests that *Atlascopcosaurus* was not always under intense pressure from predators, and that it probably did not need to migrate to avoid the harsh polar winters.

CRETACEOUS (145–65 mya)

241

TENONTOSAURUS

There is still some debate about the classification of *Tenontosaurus*. Some scientists maintain it was an advanced hypsilophodontid while others argue that it was an early iguanodontid. *Tenontosaurus* does appear to have been a transitory form between the smaller ornithopods.

TAIL HELD HIGH
Because its spinal column was almost parallel to the ground, *Tenonotosaurus* probably would have held its thick, bulky tail above the ground.

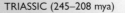

TRIASSIC (245–208 mya)   JURASSIC (208–145 mya)

FIERCE FIGHT
This reconstructed scene shows a pack of ferocious *Deinonychus* attacking a single *Tenontosaurus*.

KEY FACTS
Group Ornithopoda
Family Hypsilophodontidae
Genus *Tenontosaurus*
   ten-ON-toh-SAW-rus
Meaning Tendon lizard
Size 26 feet (8 m)
Diet Plant-eater
Hip type Ornithischian
Region Montana, Wyoming, USA
Museums Peabody Museum of Natural History, New Haven, USA; Academy of Natural Sciences, Philadelphia, USA

Discovery *Tenontosaurus* fossils have been found in the United States in Montana and Wyoming.

Characteristics The tendons running along the backbone in the hip region on *Tenontosaurus* were so well developed that they inspired the dinosaur's name. These tendons were strengthened with bone and were arranged in bundles that ran parallel to the length of the spine. As a result, the spine, from the lower back to the upper tail, would have been very stiff. This would have helped *Tenontosaurus* support the weight of its body across the hips; the torso was held stiffly in front of the hips and was balanced by the tail, which stretched out horizontally behind. Despite the advantages of having clawed feet and a huge tail, *Tenontosaurus* would have been easy prey for packs of sharp-fanged *Deinonychus*, which was its main enemy.

CRETACEOUS (145–65 mya)

MUTTABURRASAURUS

A large ornithopod that stood about 16 feet (5 m) high, *Muttaburrasaurus* is known from about 60 percent of its skeleton.

Discovery A Mr. David Langdon found the skeleton on Muttaburra Station, in northern Queensland, Australia, in 1963. A second skull, well preserved and slightly older than the original specimen, was discovered on another property in north central Queensland. A number of isolated bones and teeth of *Muttaburrasaurus* were also unearthed on the Lightning Ridge opal field in northern New South Wales.

Characteristics A distinctive feature of this dinosaur was a well-developed bump on its snout. This may have housed an acoustic organ for calling to other dinosaurs. *Muttaburrasaurus's* strong jaws and its teeth, which were suited to shearing food rather than grinding it, have led some scientists to speculate that this plant-eating dinosaur may have eaten meat from time to time.

Muttaburrasaurus *probably walked on all fours for most of the time, but it could stand up on its hindlimbs to reach high into tree branches.*

TRIASSIC (245–208 mya)   JURASSIC (208–145 mya)

The bump on the snout of this dinosaur is called a "nasal bulla."

Muttaburrasaurus had large areas of jaw muscle attachments, which greatly enhanced its chewing ability.

KEY FACTS

Group Ornithopoda
Family Euornithopoda
Genus *Muttaburrasaurus*
MUT-uh-BUH-ruh-SAW-rus
Meaning Lizard from Muttaburra
Size 33 feet (10 m)
Diet Mainly a plant-eater
Hip type Ornithischian
Region Northern Queensland and New South Wales, Australia
Museums Queensland Museum, Brisbane, Australia; Western Australian Museum, Perth, Australia

MUSEUM DISPLAY
This skeleton of *Muttaburrasaurus* is on display in the Queensland Museum in Brisbane, Australia.

TYRANNOSAURUS

Although *Tyrannosaurus rex* exemplifies for most people the very idea of a ferocious predator, fossil evidence for this animal was surprisingly scant until quite recently; it was only in the early 1990s that important gaps in our understanding were filled in.

Discovery In 1905 Henry Fairfield Osborn first described *Tyrannosaurus* from fossils that Barnum Brown had discovered in Montana. Over the years new fossil finds allowed Osborn to amplify his interpretation and gradually added to our understanding of this dinosaur. Several more complete skeletons were found. However, no hand came to light until 1990, when John Horner published an account of a specimen from Montana in which the hand was preserved. In 1991, perhaps the largest and most complete

Tyrannosaurus skeleton to date was found on a ranch in South Dakota. A legal battle over ownership followed this discovery until finally in May 2000 this skeleton, named "Sue," went on display in Chicago's Field Museum.

TRIASSIC (245–208 mya)   JURASSIC (208–145 mya)

The long, solid tail acted as a counterweight to the huge head and body.

KEY FACTS

Group Theropoda
Family Tyrannosauridae
Genus *Tyrannosaurus*
   tie-RAN-oh-SAW-rus
Meaning Tyrant lizard
Size 40 feet (12 m)
Diet Meat-eater
Hip type Saurischian
Region North America
(Canada, USA)
Museums Many museums in the USA, including: American Museum of Natural History, New York; Carnegie Museum, Pittsburgh; Field Museum, Chicago; Museum of the Rockies, Bozeman; Denver Museum of Natural History, Denver; Tyrrell Museum, Alberta, Canada; Senckenberg Museum, Frankfurt, Germany

NOTABLE FEATURES

Tyrannosaurus had huge hindlimbs, but its forelimbs were hardly longer than the forearms of an adult human. Bony protruberances above and below its eyes may have helped protect the eyes from the blows of struggling prey.

Characteristics *Tyrannosaurus*'s front teeth were D-shaped in cross-section. Each cheek bore 12 rather robust teeth, which were serrated and had a more pronounced curve than those of most other theropods. The predatory habits of this dinosaur are still unclear. Some people maintain that, because it was probably not a fast mover and because its forelimbs were tiny, it was not an active hunter, but scavenged on the dead bodies of other dinosaurs. Others, however, point to the strength of this animal's teeth and the evidence that bite marks found on *Triceratops* bones seem to have been made by *Tyrannosaurus* teeth to argue that it probably captured live prey.

MUSEUM SPECIMEN
This *Tyrannosaurus* skeleton is on display at the American Museum of Natural History in New York.

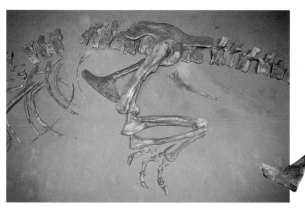

DESERT FIND
These parts of a *Tyrannosaurus* skeleton were found in the Gobi Desert in Mongolia.

BUILT FOR STRENGTH
The tibia and femur of *Tyrannosaurus* were the same length and had powerful muscles attached to them.

ALBERTOSAURUS

Albertosaurus was a slightly older relative of *Tyrannosaurus*, which it closely resembled in many respects. *Tyrannosaurus* lived between 70 and 65 million years ago; *Albertosaurus* roamed the North American late Cretaceous world between 75 and 70 million years ago.

JAWS
With its powerful jaws, *Albertosaurus* could tear off chunks of flesh from its victims.

Recent discoveries of Albertosaurus fossils include wishbones—a feature this dinosaur shared with other advanced theropods as well as with birds.

TRIASSIC (245–208 mya)   JURASSIC (208–145 mya)

Although it probably moved faster than Tyrannosaurus, Albertosaurus, *with its bulky hindlimbs, was still a relatively slow mover.*

Discovery Searches of fossil-bearing beds in south-western Alberta have yielded some remarkable finds, including a number of nearly complete skeletons of juvenile *Albertosaurus*. In some cases, several skeletons, at different stages of growth, have been found together.

Characteristics *Albertosaurus* was a huge biped with two-fingered hands and thin plates of bone covering some of its skull openings. *Albertosaurus* was smaller and had a narrower skull than *Tyrannosaurus*, and its eyes looked more to the side. In front of its eyes, *Albertosaurus* had a pair of small, blunt horns. Perhaps because its body was smaller, *Albertosaurus*'s skeleton was more gracile than that of *Tyrannosaurus*.

KEY FACTS

Group Theropoda
Family Tyrannosauridae
Genus *Albertosaurus*
    al-BERT-oh-SAW-rus
Meaning Alberta lizard
Size 26 feet (8 m)
Diet Meat-eater
Hip type Saurischian
Region South-western Canada
Museums Royal Tyrrell Museum, Alberta, Canada; Royal Ontario Museum, Toronto, Canada; American Museum of Natural History, New York, USA; Field Museum, Chicago, USA

FOSSIL FOOT
This fossil foot of *Albertosaurus* is housed in the American Museum of Natural History in New York.

CRETACEOUS (145–65 mya)

GIGANOTOSAURUS

When the discovery of *Giganotosaurus*, a dinosaur from the late Cretaceous of southern Argentina was made public, the news caused quite a sensation.

Discovery For almost a century, until the announcement in 1995, paleontologists had believed that *Tyrannosaurus* was the largest theropod. *Giganotosaurus*, however, proved to be at least as large. The first *Giganotosaurus* find consisted of an incomplete skeleton. This, however, was enough for scientists to conclude that although estimates of its size were difficult to make, it was obviously closely related to animals such as *Allosaurus*.

Characteristics In describing this dinosaur, Argentinians Rodolfo Coria and Leonardo Salgado reported a length of

41 feet (12.5 m)—longer than some *Tyrannosaurus* skeletons. Since 1995, a number of new discoveries have been made. In one case, several *Giganotosaurus* skeletons were found close together. This suggests that these dinosaurs may have moved around and hunted in groups.

TRIASSIC (245–208 mya)   JURASSIC (208–145 mya)

Giganotosaurus *had clawed three-fingered hands and clawed three-toed feet.*

EDUCATED GUESSWORK

This reconstruction of *Giganotosaurus* was made using evidence from skeletal remains and by making educated guesses based on the internal organs of living relatives, such as crocodiles and birds. Some missing tail bones in skeletons of *Giganotosaurus* were modeled on those of close relatives such as *Allosaurus*.

KEY FACTS
Group Theropoda
Family Allosauroidea
Genus *Giganotosaurus*
  JIG-an-oh-toh-SAW-rus
Meaning Giant southern lizard
Size 43 feet (13 m)
Diet Meat-eater
Hip type Saurischian
Region Patagonia, Argentina
Museums Academy of Natural Sciences, Philadelphia, USA

CRETACEOUS (145–65 mya)

SPINOSAURUS

Spinosaurus, a theropod that lived in the late Cretaceous, was so named because of the extremely tall spines on its vertebrae.

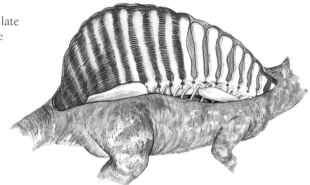

Discovery At the beginning of the 20th century, the German paleontologist Ernst Freiherr Stromer von Reichenbach discovered the remains of several formerly unknown late Cretaceous dinosaurs in Egypt in the western Sahara Desert. The most significant of these finds was *Spinosaurus*. Stromer collected some fragmentary remains of this dinosaur in 1912 and described it in 1914. Sadly, Stromer's *Spinosaurus* specimen, as well as those of other Egyptian dinosaurs he discovered, were destroyed during World War II. Fortunately for science, Stromer published a detailed description of the material he collected.

Characteristics In many ways, *Spinosaurus* resembled a number of other theropods, such as *Allosaurus*. Unlike other spinosaurids, it had huge neural spines on its vertebrae which formed a sail over the back. This sail may have been used as a heat regulator, a signaling device or as a means of sexual display.

COOLING PLANT
Spinosaurus's sail may have acted like a built-in cooling plant. When things got too hot, the dinosaur may have stood in the shade and pumped warm blood into the sail, where the blood cooled down before going back into the body.

TRIASSIC (245–208 mya)   JURASSIC (208–145 mya)

Long bones held up the huge sail on the back of Spinosaurus.

Scientists suspect that Spinosaurus's sail, which rose to more than 5 feet (1.5 m) high, was probably covered with skin.

The teeth of Spinosaurus were conical and straight, unlike the curved teeth of most other theropods.

KEY FACTS
Group Theropoda
Family Spinosauridae
Genus *Spinosaurus*
   SPY-noh-SAW-rus
Meaning Spiny lizard
Size 33 feet (10 m)
Diet Meat-eater
Hip type Saurischian
Region North Africa (Egypt, Niger)
Museums Not on display

CRETACEOUS (145–65 mya)

GALLIMIMUS

Gallimimus was one of the largest, and best known of the ornithomimids, or "bird mimic" dinosaurs. It was typically found along with large tyrannosaurid theropods and duckbills, but not with the horned ceratopsians.

Discovery *Gallimimus* was discovered by the joint Polish–Mongolian expeditions to Mongolia during the 1960s, and skeletons from several stages of this dinosaur's growth have now been collected.

Characteristics *Gallimimus's* arms had much freedom of movement, although they do not seem to have been able to reach very high. To compensate for this, its long neck could probably have stretched down, allowing *Gallimimus* to bring food items from its hands up to its mouth.

This dinosaur probably fed on small animals and, perhaps, insects. It may also have eaten plants. *Gallimimus's* limbs were very long and slender and the bones of its palm—the metacarpals—were particularly long. Its hands, which were more suited for digging than grasping, may also have scooped up the eggs of other dinosaurs from the soil. It then cracked them open with the broad beak at the tip of its long snout. *Gallimimus* and the other ornithomimids were capable of great bursts of speed.

NECK AND HEAD
Gallimimus's neck was extremely long, but its skull was relatively small. The jaws were toothless.

256

TRIASSIC (245–208 mya)   JURASSIC (208–145 mya)

The tail and the neck together accounted for more than two-thirds of Gallimimus's total length.

KEY FACTS

Group Theropoda

Family Ornithomimidae

Genus *Gallimimus*
GAL-ee-MY-mus

Meaning Chicken mimic

Size 10 feet (3 m)

Diet Meat-eater. Possibly also a plant-eater

Hip type Saurischian

Region Mongolia

Museums Paleontological Museum, Mongolian Academy of Sciences, Ulan Baatar, Mongolia

CRETACEOUS (145–65 mya)

STRUTHIOMIMUS

Named for its similarity to a present-day ostrich, this long-necked, long-legged theropod is, along with the Mongolian *Gallimimus*, one of the best-known ornithomimids, or "bird mimic" dinosaurs.

Struthiomimus could have used its long, hooklike claws for digging small prey out of shallow burrows or for pulling leaves and fruit from low trees.

Discovery First described in 1902, *Struthiomimus* fossils have been found in Alberta, Canada.

Characteristics With its small and very lightly built skull, toothless beak and very large eyes, *Struthiomimus* bore a striking similarity to today's flightless birds. The three large, clawed, forward-facing toes on each of its feet were typical of theropod feet, but they were also very birdlike. Ornithomimids lacked true feathers and may have had naked skin. However, some juveniles may have had a partial covering of downy filaments similar to those that have been found on other birdlike dinosaurs. The head and beak suggest that this dinosaur could not have killed large animals, but it could have swallowed small reptiles and large insects. However, gizzard stones (gastroliths) that have been found at the front of the rib cage show that plant material was an important component of *Struthiomimus*'s diet. As well, its long neck was suited to reaching up into tree branches.

TRIASSIC (245–208 mya)   JURASSIC (208–145 mya)

Running on its long, slender back legs, Struthiomimus could reach speeds of about 50 miles per hour (80 km/h).

KEY FACTS
Group Theropoda
Family Ornithomimidae
Genus *Struthiomimus*
    STROO-thee-oh-MY-mus
Meaning Ostrich mimic
Size 13 feet (4 m)
Diet Plant-eater. Possibly also a meat-eater
Hip type Saurischian
Region Alberta, Canada
Museums Royal Tyrrell Museum, Alberta, Canada

SKELETONS
Struthiomimus was long known only from a single complete and several partial skeletons. More recently, however, a number of complete skeletons have come to light.

CRETACEOUS (145–65 mya)

OVIRAPTOR

Oviraptor is known only from the late Cretaceous of Mongolia, but other *Oviraptor*-like animals are known from the Cretaceous of other parts of Asia and western North America.

EGG ROBBER
Many paleontologists still believe that *Oviraptor* probably stole eggs from the nests of other dinosaurs. Its clawed hands would certainly have been capable of grasping these eggs.

Discovery When *Oviraptor* was found in the 1920s during an American expedition to Mongolia, most of the specimens were near nests of dinosaur eggs. It was assumed that *Oviraptor* was stealing the eggs. Later, in the 1990s, another expedition found more of the same kinds of eggs— some of them with embryos. These, they discovered, were embryos of *Oviraptor*, not of its prey. Soon after that, fossils were found of *Oviraptor* skeletons sitting on nests of their own eggs. It seems *Oviraptor* may have been named for a crime that it did not commit.

Characteristics *Oviraptor* had a short snout, toothless jaws and a rounded mass of thin bone over its nose, rather like a chicken's comb. It was one of the most birdlike of the nonavian dinosaurs. Its rib cage in particular displayed several features that are typical of birds, including a set of processes on each rib that would have kept the rib cage rigid.

260

TRIASSIC (245–208 mya)   JURASSIC (208–145 mya)

Oviraptor's long tail accounted for about half its total length.

Oviraptor's slender hind legs suggest that it was a fast mover.

KEY FACTS

Group Theropoda

Family Oviraptoridae

Genus *Oviraptor*
    oh-vee-RAP-tuh

Meaning Egg robber

Size 10 feet (3 m)

Diet Meat-eater

Hip type Saurischian

Region Mongolia

Museums American Museum of Natural History, New York, USA; Paleontological Museum, Mongolian Academy of Sciences, Ulan Baatar, Mongolia

DIFFERENT CRESTS

Crests were diverse and changed constantly during a dinosaur's lifetime. Two species of *Oviraptor*—*O. mongoliensis* (top) and *O. philoceratops* (bottom)—display different-shaped crests.

TROÖDON

For some time *Troödon* was thought to be a meat-eating ornithopod—its teeth resembled those of some ornithopods. Eventually it was recognized to be a small birdlike theropod.

Troödon's very large eyes have led some scientists to believe that this animal may have been nocturnal.

The claw on Troödon's second toe was longer than those on the other toes, but this dinosaur lacked the "killer" sickle that characterized dromaeosaurids such as Velociraptor.

TRIASSIC (245–208 mya)

JURASSIC (208–145 mya)

Discovery On the basis of a single tooth discovered in 1854 in the Judith River Formation in Alberta, Canada, Joseph Leidy described and named *Troödon* in 1856. Leidy, however, thought this animal was a lizard. Later discoveries of teeth from the late Cretaceous of Montana confirmed *Troödon* to be a dinosaur.

Characteristics Thanks to the discovery of a number of sometimes fragmentary skulls and skeletons, we know that *Troödon* had a long snout. However, instead of the row of long, curved teeth that typified most theropods, *Troödon* had a large number of relatively small teeth. Each side of the lower jaw may have had up to 35 teeth, all with large serrations and varying in size depending on where they were in the jaw. No other theropod is known to have had so many teeth. *Troödon* is famous for the size of its brain cavity. *Troödon* and other troödontids may have had the largest brains, relative to body size, of any nonavian dinosaurs. This has led some to believe that *Troödon* was more intelligent than other dinosaurs.

KEY FACTS
Group Theropoda
Family Troödontidae
Genus *Troödon*
   TROO-oh-don
Meaning Wounding tooth
Size 10 feet (3 m)
Diet Meat-eater
Hip type Saurischian
Region North-western North America
Museums Museum of the Rockies, Bozeman, USA

FIRST FIND
The first fossil of *Troödon* to be found was a single leaf-shaped tooth.

VELOCIRAPTOR

Velociraptor is the nightmarish villain of the movie *Jurassic Park*. Swift, birdlike and intelligent—as presented on screen, it embodies all the dynamic qualities that, until quite recently, dinosaurs were thought to lack.

Discovery *Velociraptor* fossils are dated from the late Cretaceous of Mongolia.

Characteristics Although in life *Velociraptor* was most likely a swift-running predator, the real animal differed in several ways from its cinematic namesake. For one thing, the skull was narrower than was depicted on screen. In fact, the heads of the movie "raptors" more closely resemble that of *Deinonychus*. The tail, too, was different. *Velociraptor* was a dromaeosaurid. Their tails were stiff, and not flexible as they were

shown in the movie. Most important is the question of size. The real *Velociraptor* was a mere 3 feet (1 m) long; in the movie, it was shown to be the size of an adult human. Like other dromaeosaurids, *Velociraptor* probably used its hooked talon to kill its prey. One celebrated *Velociraptor* skeleton, found in 1971, was entangled with a *Protoceratops* skeleton, the *Velociraptor*'s foot claw embedded in the other dinosaur's rib cage.

PREDATORS AND PREY
In this reconstructed scene from the late Cretaceous in Mongolia, a *Velociraptor* slays a *Protoceratops*, while a *Prenocephale* looks on.

TRIASSIC (245–208 mya)	JURASSIC (208–145 mya)

KEY FACTS

Group Theropoda

Family Dromaeosauridae

Genus *Velociraptor*
vel-oss-ee-RAP-tuh

Meaning Fast robber

Size 3 feet (1 m)

Diet Meat-eater

Hip type Saurischian

Region Mongolia

Museums Paleontological Museum, Mongolian Academy of Sciences, Ulan Baatar, Mongolia; American Museum of Natural History, New York, USA; Paleontological Institute, Moscow, Russia

As well as the deadly sickle claw on each of its feet, Velociraptor had needle-sharp claws at the ends of its long fingers.

DROMAEOSAURUS

New evidence of *Dromaeosaurus* has come
to light in recent years, but the scarceness
of its fossil remains suggest that it may have
been a rare theropod.

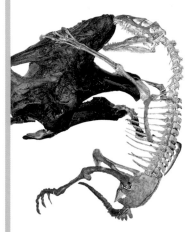

Discovery Although until
recently *Dromaeosaurus* was
known almost exclusively from a
skull and some fragmentary bones
found by Barnum Brown in 1914
in Alberta, Canada, it has given its
name to a dinosaur family—the
dromaeosaurids.

LETHAL COMBAT
In this reconstruction, a
Dromaeosaurus launches an
attack with its teeth and
claws on the largest of the
hadrosaurs, *Lambeosaurus*.

Characteristics *Dromaeosaurus*,
like all dromaeosaurids, had an
extremely stiff tail. The tails of
most theropods were stiffened, at
least for part of their length. This
was caused by the lengthening of
the attachment processes (bony
rods known as zygapophyses) on
the vertebrae. In dromaeosaurids,
these rods were greatly elongated,
each of them extending over
several vertebrae and bracing them
solidly together. This stiff tail
would have helped *Dromaeosaurus*
in pursuing prey by acting as a
counterbalance behind the hip.

TRIASSIC (245–208 mya)   JURASSIC (208–145 mya)

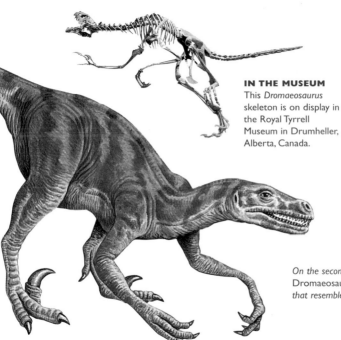

KEY FACTS

Group Theropoda

Family Dromaeosauridae

Genus *Dromaeosaurus*
   droh-MAY-oh-SAW-rus

Meaning Running lizard

Size 6 feet (1.8 m)

Diet Meat-eater

Hip type Saurischian

Region Alberta, Canada

Museums Royal Tyrrell Museum,
Alberta, Canada

IN THE MUSEUM
This *Dromaeosaurus* skeleton is on display in the Royal Tyrrell Museum in Drumheller, Alberta, Canada.

On the second toe of each foot, Dromaeosaurus *had a deadly claw that resembled a switchblade.*

MONONYKUS

The discoverers of *Mononykus* first thought they had discovered a primitive bird, and some recent analyses suggest that it was a very close relative of birds. However, it is clear from the animal's skeletal structure that *Mononykus* was probably not capable of flight.

Discovery *Mononykus* was found in joint Mongolian–American expeditions to Mongolia in the mid-1990s. As other alvarezsaurids are known from the Cretaceous of North and South America, the find in distant Mongolia suggests that members of this family could have occurred worldwide.

Characteristics *Mononykus* was powerfully built—the construction of the elbows suggests the existence of large extension muscles. Most small theropods had long forelimbs and long, grasping hands. However,

Mononykus and its closest relatives were conspicuous exceptions to this rule. *Mononykus*'s forelimbs were, in fact, too short to reach its face. In some ways they resemble the forelimbs of digging mammals such as moles. It has been suggested that *Mononykus* may have been a digging animal that used these arms to rip open termite mounds. Perhaps it was, but the rest of the skeleton is absolutely unlike that of any known burrowing animal.

Mononykus's legs resembled those of birds in that the fibula did not reach right down to the ankle.

TRIASSIC (245–208 mya)   JURASSIC (208–145 mya)

Scientists think that Mononykus *probably had thin fibers that may have been primitive feathers around parts of its body.*

KEY FACTS
Group Theropoda
Family Alvarezsauridae
Genus *Mononykus*
mon-oh-NIE-kus
Meaning One claw
Size 3 feet (1 m)
Diet Meat-eater
Hip type Saurischian
Region Mongolia
Museums American Museum of
Natural History, New York, USA

ARM AND HAND STRUCTURE
Mononykus had extremely short, but sturdy, arms, and a hand that consisted almost entirely of the single-clawed digit for which the dinosaur is named.

CRETACEOUS (145–65 mya)

SEGNOSAURUS

Few dinosaurs have caused as much debate as *Segnosaurus*. It displayed an unusual collection of characteristics that resembled bits of many other dinosaurs and groups, combined with some features found only in *Segnosaurus* and its close relatives, the segnosaurs.

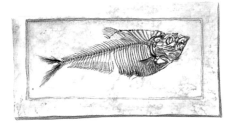

Discovery *Segnosaurus* was described in 1979, and is known only from fragments and isolated bones, found in late Cretaceous deposits of Mongolia and China.

Characteristics The front of *Segnosaurus*'s snout was toothless and may have supported a beak, as in some ornithischian dinosaurs. *Segnosaurus*'s hip arrangement was similar to that of the ornithischians. The current consensus, however, is that *Segnosaurus* and its relatives form a strange group of theropods. Features they share include toes and fingers with curved claws and a high, narrow skull. Curiously, the jaw curved downward and had small pointed teeth along each side. It has been suggested that *Segnosaurus* was a herbivore descended from a carnivore, a specialist termite hunter, or, alternatively, that it snatched fish from the water with its huge claws.

FISH FOSSILS
Segnosaurus's diet remains something of a mystery. However, it may well have been predominantly a fish-eater that consumed prey like the fish shown here in fossilized form.

TRIASSIC (245–208 mya)   JURASSIC (208–145 mya)

KEY FACTS
Group Segnosauria
Family Therizinosauridae
Genus *Segnosaurus*
SEG-noh-SAW-rus
Meaning Slow lizard
Size 19 feet 6 inches (6 m)
Diet Plant- or meat-eater, or both
Hip type Similar to that of
ornithischians
Region Mongolia
Museums Paleontological Museum,
Mongolian Academy of Sciences, Ulan
Baatar, Mongolia

Segnosaurus *had three-fingered
hands and four-toed feet.*

CRETACEOUS (145–65 mya)

SALTASAURUS

Saltasaurus comes from rock laid down near the end of the age of the dinosaurs. While sauropods dominated the late Jurassic, they were scarce for most of the Cretaceous. *Saltasaurus* and its kin, the titanosaurids, seem to have been making a late reappearance.

Discovery *Saltasaurus* was first described in 1980 by Argentinian paleontologist José Bonaparte. Several specimens of *Saltasaurus* have been found, representing three species. Most of the skeleton is known. However, most of the skull and many of the foot bones remain to be discovered.

Characteristics *Saltasaurus* was the first armored sauropod to be found. The armor comprised bony studs that inter-connected to form a shield over the back. *Saltasaurus*'s tail was long and ended in a whiplike lash similar to that of *Diplodocus*. The bones of the tail interlocked, thus stiffening the whole structure and possibly providing support for the animal when it reared up on its hind legs.

BONY ARMOR
The bony studs that covered the back of *Saltasaurus* varied greatly in size, but did not exhibit any formal pattern.

272

TRIASSIC (245–208 mya)   JURASSIC (208–145 mya)

KEY FACTS
Group Sauropoda
Family Titanosauridae
Genus *Saltasaurus*
   SALT-uh-SAW-rus
Meaning Salta lizard
Size 39 feet (12 m)
Diet Plant-eater
Hip type Saurischian
Region Salta, Rionegro, Argentina; Palmitas, Uruguay
Museums Argentine Museum of Natural Sciences, Buenos Aires, Argentina

By sauropod standards, Saltasaurus was quite stocky, and had relatively short, stumpy hind legs.

EDMONTONIA

Edmontonia was one of the largest nodosaurids, one of the two main groups of armored ankylosaurs. *Edmontonia* was one of the last of this group, appearing late in the age of dinosaurs.

HEAD AND SHOULDERS
Edmontonia could tuck its head below its huge shoulder spikes and drive them forward with lethal effect into the body of an attacker. Its head was boxy, with a cropping beak at the front of the mouth.

TRIASSIC (245–208 mya)   JURASSIC (208–145 mya)

SOLID PROTECTION
Edmontonia's armor plating formed an impenetrable shield against attack. Even the head was covered with bony plates.

KEY FACTS
Group Ankylosauria
Family Nodosauridae
Genus *Edmontonia*
    ed-mon-TOH-nee-ah
Meaning Of Edmonton
Size 23 feet (7 m)
Diet Plant-eater
Hip type Ornithischian
Region Alberta, Canada; Montana, Texas, USA
Museums Royal Tyrrell Museum, Alberta, Canada

Discovery *Edmontonia* fossils have been found in Alberta, Canada and Texas and Montana in the United States.

Characteristics Nodosaurids such as *Edmontonia* had a boxlike head and bony armor covering the neck, back and upper surfaces of the tail. The armor consisted of three types of bony elements embedded in the skin. The largest were pronounced spikes, on the shoulders and forming two rows running along the sides. Also, there were shieldlike scutes of varying sizes and, in between, thousands of pea-sized ossicles. As with other nodosaurids, *Edmontonia*'s belly was unprotected by armor and would have been vulnerable if the animal were tipped over. To protect against this, the body was very low-slung, with relatively short, stumpy legs spread wide by broad hips and shoulder girdles.

CRETACEOUS (145–65 mya)

ANKYLOSAURUS

The last and largest of all the armored dinosaurs, *Ankylosaurus* gives its name to its group—the ankylosaurs—and takes its name from the bony nature of its skeleton. "Ankylosed" means "stiffened with bone."

Discovery *Ankylosaurus* was found and named by the famous American paleontologist Barnum Brown in some of the very youngest beds that contain dinosaur fossils.

Characteristics The back and tail of *Ankylosaurus* were covered by interlocking bony shields, and the vertebrae at the end of the tail were welded together by bone. Just like its close relative *Euoplocephalus*, *Ankylosaurus* had a complex system of loops and twists in its nasal passages, but the function these served is not clear.

They may have been for warming air, or for collecting moisture from air being exhaled. They may have been lined with sensors that enhanced the animal's sense of smell for detecting food, predators or potential mates. It is also possible that they were used as a resonating chamber, helping *Ankylosaurus* to make loud mating or distress calls.

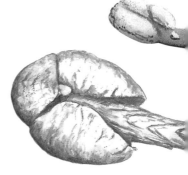

Ankylosaurus's *head, as well as its body, was covered by layers of bony plates and spikes.*

SWINGING PERIL
Ankylosaurus could swing its massive tail club around to do serious harm to an intending predator.

TRIASSIC (245–208 mya)   JURASSIC (208–145 mya)

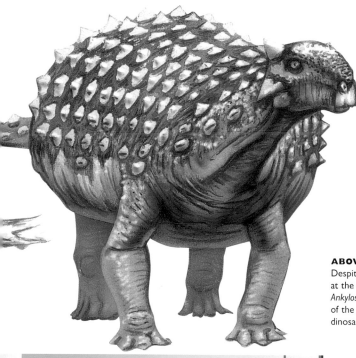

KEY FACTS

Group Thyreophora
Family Ankylosauridae
Genus *Ankylosaurus*
    an-KEE-loh-SAW-rus
Meaning Stiff lizard
Size 33 feet (10 m)
Diet Plant-eater
Hip type Ornithischian
Region Montana, Wyoming, USA;
Alberta, Canada
Museums Provincial Museum of
Alberta, Edmonton, Canada; American
Museum of Natural History,
New York, USA

ABOVE GROUND

Despite its weight and its position
at the end of a long, heavy tail,
Ankylosaurus's tail club was carried clear
of the ground. Trackways made by this
dinosaur show no sign of a tail dragging.

CRETACEOUS (145–65 mya)

EDMONTOSAURUS

Edmontosaurus was one of the last hadrosaurids, and also one of the largest. As well, along with *Tyrannosaurus* and *Triceratops*, it was one of the last surviving dinosaurs, living right to the end of the Cretaceous period.

The spine of this dinosaur was supported by huge bony tendons, which criss-crossed all the way down.

Edmontosaurus *had padded hooves on its forelimbs.*

TRIASSIC (245–208 mya)   JURASSIC (208–145 mya)

PLUCKING FOOD

Like all hadrosaurs, *Edmontosaurus* had a toothless duckbill, covered with skin, which it used to pluck leaves and fruits. Its teeth were in the back of its mouth.

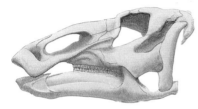

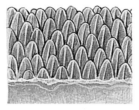

TIGHT PACKING

Edmontosaurus's jaws contained tightly packed rows of tiny leaf-shaped teeth that were ideal for grinding.

KEY FACTS

Group Ornithopoda

Family Hadrosauridae

Genus *Edmontosaurus*
ed-MON-toh-SAW-rus

Meaning Edmonton lizard

Size 42 feet (13 m)

Diet Plant-eater

Hip type Ornithischian

Region Alberta, Canada

Museums Peabody Museum of Natural History, New Haven, USA; Smithsonian Institution, Washington DC, USA; Royal Ontario Museum, Toronto, Canada

Discovery Spectacular finds of this dinosaur from Alberta, Canada have preserved impressions of the skin around parts of the body, including the "hand."

Characteristics *Edmontosaurus* was a huge animal. It could have weighed up to 5 tons (5.1 tonnes).

It probably moved about on all fours, rising up on its back legs only when it needed to run. It was one of the "mummified" fossils that led to early reconstructions of hadrosaurids as mainly aquatic animals. It was realized later that what looked like webbing between the fingers was really the remains of padding behind the hooves. Many modern hoofed animals have similar padding, which helps to bear the animal's weight. *Edmontosaurus* and other hadrosaurids are now always represented in reconstructions as fully terrestrial animals.

CRETACEOUS (145–65 mya)

MAIASAURA

Some paleontologists believe that *Maiasaura* were strongly social animals that lived in the late Cretaceous period in herds of many thousands.

Like all hadrosaurs, Maiasaura had a horny, toothless beak at the front of its mouth.

Discovery The first fossils ever found of *Maiasaura* were a huge nesting colony, about 75 million years old. It was discovered in the badlands of Montana in 1978 by John Horner and Robert Makela. This colony contained eggs (many still intact), babies and adults; even the way the eggs were arranged could be seen. This seeming demonstration of parental care inspired the name of this dinosaur.

Characteristics The proximity of the nests suggests that females nested in large groups. Careful study of the site led to some interesting insights into the nurturing habits of *Maiasaura*. Many of these babies were clearly too large to be newly hatched but were evidently still living in the nest. Like the leg bones of some species of modern birds, the bones in the legs of the baby *Maiasaura* were not fully formed. Despite this, their teeth showed signs of wear. The logical conclusion was that the babies were being fed in the nest.

TRIASSIC (245–208 mya)   JURASSIC (208–145 mya)

JUVENILE DINOSAUR

This is a reconstructed skeleton of a juvenile *Maiasaura*. As the animals grew, their heads became flatter and wider.

KEY FACTS

Group Ornithopoda
Family Hadrosauridae
Genus *Maiasaura*
   MY-uh-SAW-rah
Meaning Good mother lizard
Size 30 feet (9 m)
Diet Plant-eater
Hip type Ornithischian
Region Montana, USA
Museums Museum of the Rockies, Bozeman, USA

EMBRYO

This is a *Maiasaura* embryo at an advanced stage of development. The yolk sac, shown here in yellow, provided nourishment for the unhatched infant.

CORYTHOSAURUS

Corythosaurus, the best known of the crested duckbill dinosaurs (lambeosaurine hadrosaurs), lived beside the ancient inland sea of western North America in the late Cretaceous period.

Discovery *Corythosaurus* fossils have been found in Alberta, Canada and Montana in the United States.

Characteristics Most of the body weight of *Corythosaurus* was supported by the large three-toed hindlimbs and balanced by the large tail. Criss-crossing ossified tendons stiffened the tail all the way from the hips, preventing the tail from swinging when the dinosaur ran. Like other duckbills, this dinosaur had huge numbers of teeth crammed together to form a single grinding surface on each side of the upper and lower jaws. The most distinctive feature of

lambeosaurines was the hollow bony crest on top of the head. The size and shape of these crests varied greatly, because the crests changed as they grew and differed between the sexes. Adult males probably had the largest crests, which they used in behavioral displays to attract mates and to intimidate other males. *Corythosaurus* walked on all fours, using flattened, blunt claws on its four-fingered hands.

TRIASSIC (245–208 mya)   JURASSIC (208–145 mya)

The spine of *Corythosaurus* was flexed, or "hunched," at the shoulders, which suggested that this dinosaur fed mainly on low-growing plants.

KEY FACTS

Group Ornithopoda

Family Hadrosauridae

Genus *Corythosaurus*
koh-RITH-oh-SAW-rus

Meaning Corinthian-crested lizard

Size 33 feet (10 m)

Diet Plant-eater

Hip type Ornithischian

Region Alberta, Canada;
Montana, USA

Museums American Museum of
Natural History, New York, USA;
Royal Ontario Museum, Toronto,
Canada

DUCKBILL SKULL

Corythosaurus tore off leaves with its horny beak, stored them in its cheek pouches, then ground them with rows of strong, interlocking teeth.

CRETACEOUS (145–65 mya)

LAMBEOSAURUS

One of the largest of the crested duckbill dinosaurs, *Lambeosaurus* lived in the same area and at the same time as several other members of this group of low-browsing herbivores. It seems, in fact, that several species of *Lambeosaurus* lived at the same time.

Discovery Nearly 20 skulls and skeletons of *Lambeosaurus* have been described from the late Cretaceous period.

Characteristics One fossil deposit, a "bonebed" containing hundreds of jumbled-up skeletons buried by floods, includes specimens of *Lambeosaurus*, along with *Corythosaurus* and several other crested duckbills. This suggests that these duckbills shared the same habitat and may have migrated in huge mixed herds. Different species of *Lambeosaurus* were distinguished by different-shaped bony crests on the tops of their heads. The hollow crest would have formed a resonating chamber for its calls, amplifying them and making a distinctive sound in each species. The shape and patterning of the crest would have helped individuals to recognize each other in the herd.

PLANT-EATING APPARATUS
Lambeosaurus had a beak for breaking off leaves and fruit, and teeth at the back for grinding. As the teeth wore out, they were replaced.

284

TRIASSIC (245–208 mya)   JURASSIC (208–145 mya)

KEY FACTS

Group Ornithopoda
Family Hadrosauridae
Genus *Lambeosaurus*
   LAM-bee-oh-SAW-rus
Meaning Lambe's lizard
Size 49 feet (15 m)
Diet Plant-eater
Hip type Ornithischian
Region Alberta, Canada; Montana, USA; Baja California, Mexico
Museums Royal Tyrrell Museum, Alberta, Canada

LOW BROWSER

Lambeosaurus usually browsed near the ground while standing on all fours, but it was also capable of moving on its hindlimbs. Like *Edmontosaurus* and *Corythosaurus*, *Lambeosaurus* had hooves on its forelimbs.

CRETACEOUS (145–65 mya)

SAUROLOPHUS

The most distinctive feature of *Saurolophus* was the sharp, pointed ridge of bone that projected from the top of its head. This large hadrosaur is now known from several well-preserved, complete skeletons.

Discovery The first species to be discovered, *Saurolophus osborni*, was named by Barnum Brown in 1921. It was found in the Horseshoe Canyon Formation of southern Alberta, Canada. The other, and larger, species (most commonly found in Mongolia) is *S. angustirostris*, which was named by the Russian paleontologist A. Rozhdestvensky in 1952. Except for some differences in the overall size and in the shape and height of the crest, the two species of *Saurolophus* are almost identical. This suggests that by the end of the Cretaceous, this dinosaur was widely distributed across the Northern Hemisphere.

Characteristics The pointed ridge on *Saurolophus*'s head may have been covered by fleshy nostrils or flaps. *Saurolophus* had large numbers of closely packed teeth in the back of its mouth. These were well suited to chewing the tough plant material, such as ferns and conifers, that constituted this dinosaur's diet. *Saurolophus* sheared off this plant matter with the horny beak at the tip of its snout.

INFLATED CREST
Saurolophus may have been able to inflate the skin that covered its crest in order to make sounds or as a form of courtship display.

TRIASSIC (245–208 mya)   JURASSIC (208–145 mya)

Surviving skin impressions indicate that Saurolophus had leathery, fine-scaled skin.

KEY FACTS

Group Ornithopoda
Family Hadrosauridae
Genus *Saurolophus*
  SAW-roh-LOW-fus
Meaning Ridged lizard
Size 42 feet (13 m)
Diet Plant-eater
Hip type Ornithischian
Region Alberta, Canada; Mongolia
Museums American Museum of
Natural History, New York, USA;
Paleontological Institute,
Moscow, Russia

It is possible that colored skin covered Saurolophus's crest and stretched between the crest and the back of the head.

CRETACEOUS (145–65 mya)

287

PARASAUROLOPHUS

With its snout drawn up into a giant snorkel-like structure, *Parasaurolophus* was one of the most bizarre of all the hadrosaurs. The main dangers that *Parasaurolophus* faced were from larger predators such as *Albertosaurus*. It probably sought protection by living in large herds, just as herbivores on the African plains do today.

Although it moved mainly on all fours, this dinosaur could stand up on its broad, three-toed back feet.

TOOTHLESS BEAK
The front of the snout formed a toothless beak, shaped like a duck's bill, for pecking at leaves and fruit.

TRIASSIC (245–208 mya)   JURASSIC (208–145 mya)

Discovery Levi Sternberg collected the first skeleton of *Parasaurolophus* in 1921 in the region of southern Alberta, Canada, that is now the Dinosaur Provincial Park.

Characteristics Like all hadrosaurs, *Parasaurolophus* was a plant-eater. It had many closely compacted teeth, each of which had a central ridge. These teeth formed a strong dental battery that made it possible for this dinosaur to chew tough vegetable matter. *Parasaurolophus* lacked a hole in its apex, and therefore it is clear that the bony, snorkel-like structure was not used, as has been suggested, for breathing while the animal was swimming or feeding underwater. It seems likely that it helped this dinosaur produce noises for signaling to mates or, if it was colored, for courtship displays. We know from the specimens that have been discovered that soft tissues adorned the bony crest. The internal structure of the crest had a hollow area that connected with the nostrils and the back of the throat

KEY FACTS

Group Ornithopoda

Family Hadrosauridae

Genus *Parasaurolophus*
PAR-uh-SAW-roh-LOH-fus

Meaning Side-ridged lizard

Size 35 feet (10.5 m)

Diet Plant-eater

Hip type Ornithischian

Region Montana, New Mexico, USA; Alberta, Canada

Museums Royal Ontario Museum, Ontario, Canada; Los Angeles County Museum, USA

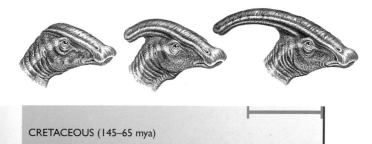

TELLING THEM APART

Scientists now generally think that different crests on *Parasaurolophus* distinguished males from females and adults from juveniles. Juveniles (far left) had the shortest crests, adult females (center) had longer crests, while adult males (near left) had the longest crests.

CRETACEOUS (145–65 mya)

289

CARCHARODONTOSAURUS

This huge north African dinosaur, whose head was as large as that of *Tyrannosaurus*, but whose brain cavity was much smaller, was a close relative of *Giganotosaurus* from South America.

NAMING A DINOSAUR
Carcharodontosaurus was named because its teeth were thought to resemble those of a modern great white shark, the generic name for which is *Carcharodon*.

290

TRIASSIC (245–208 mya)   JURASSIC (208–145 mya)

Carcharodontosaurus's snout was deep and domed and its jaws were driven by powerful muscles.

KEY FACTS

Group Theropoda

Family Allosauroidae

Genus *Carcharodontosaurus*
kuh-KAR-oh-dont-oh-SAW-rus

Meaning White-shark-toothed lizard

Size 43 feet (13 m)

Diet Meat-eater

Hip type Saurischian

Region North Africa

Museums Not on display

Discovery The German Ernst Freiherr Stromer von Reichenbach first described *Carcharodontosaurus* in the 1930s, and he was the first to remark on the sharklike nature of its teeth. This observed similarity led to the naming of this dinosaur.

Characteristics Like other theropods, *Carcharodontosaurus* had teeth that were serrated along the front and back. However, these teeth were triangular and did not curve back as much as those of most theropods. Both had similar snouts and teeth that were smaller and more numerous than those of *Tyrannosaurus*. It is quite possible that these two contemporaneous, but geographically separated, dinosaurs shared a common ancestor that lived at a time when Africa and South America were still parts of the same landmass. When this landmass broke apart, different lineages could have developed. Like *Giganotosaurus*, *Carcharodontosaurus* may have preyed on large sauropods.

CRETACEOUS (145–65 mya)

STYGIMOLOCH

Stygimoloch lived in a lowland habitat, where the principal predators would have been large theropods such as *Tyrannosaurus*, *Albertosaurus* and *Aublysodon*.

Discovery *Stygimoloch* was found in, and named for, the Hell Creek site in Montana in the United States.

Characteristics What we know about this elusive plant-eater has been gleaned from only about five skull fragments and parts of the body skeleton. With well-developed horns and spikes protruding from the base of its domed skull and from its snout, *Stygimoloch* was more elaborately ornamented than most pachycephalosaurs. Males may have used these horns for locking heads with opponents in head-pushing contests for winning mates. The horns, which were not very strong, may, on the other hand, have been purely ornamental and used only for courtship displays. Because fossil remains of *Stygimoloch* are so scarce, our understanding of this dinosaur is still very limited. Those parts of the skull that scientists have been able to study show that the holes in the rear of the skull roofs of many pachycephalosaurs (known as the "temporal fenestrae") had closed up in *Stygimoloch*. This suggests that this dinosaur was one of the more advanced of the pachycephalosaurs.

STRONG SKULL
Stygimoloch's solid skull was more robust than those of many pachycephalosaurs. The horns, however, were relatively fragile.

TRIASSIC (245–208 mya)   JURASSIC (208–145 mya)

KEY FACTS

Group Ornithopoda
Family Pachycephalosauridae
Genus *Stygimoloch*
    STY-gee-MOH-lok
Meaning River of Hell devil
Size 20 feet (6 m)
Diet Plant-eater
Hip type Ornithischian
Region Wyoming, Montana, USA
Museums Not on display

Stygimoloch *walked upright, and had relatively small forelimbs.*

CRETACEOUS (145–65 mya)

PROTOCERATOPS

One of the earliest of the ceratopsian dinosaurs, *Protoceratops* was a very common animal in the late Cretaceous lowland habitats of Mongolia.

The size and weight of Protoceratops's head and jaws ensured that this dinosaur moved about on all fours.

Discovery Fossilized remains of *Protoceratops* were among the most abundant fossils found on the American expeditions to Mongolia that Roy Chapman Andrews led between 1922 and 1925.

Characteristics The abundance of these fossils has led scientists to believe that *Protoceratops* was a highly social animal that lived in herds. *Protoceratops* had a large frill that extended back from the face and over the neck. However, it lacked the horns of the more advanced ceratopsians, although some species featured a small bump on the snout that may have

supported a keratinous horn, similar to that of a rhinoceros. Thanks to the abundance of skulls of *Protoceratops*, scientists have detected differences between the sexes. In adult males, the frill was more erect and there was a more prominent bump on the snout. This suggests that males used the larger frill and snout bump as a device to attract females. The bump may also have been used in fights between rival males.

TRIASSIC (245–208 mya)   JURASSIC (208–145 mya)

SHARP IMPLEMENTS
Protoceratops had a parrotlike beak for shearing off plant stems and scissorlike teeth to slice up its food.

KEY FACTS

Group Ceratopsia
Family Protoceratopsidae
Genus *Protoceratops*
  PROH-toh-SAIR-uh-tops
Meaning First-horned face
Size 10 feet (3 m)
Diet Plant-eater
Hip type Ornithischian
Region Mongolia; China; Canada
Museums American Museum of Natural History, New York, USA; Paleontological Museum, Moscow, Russia; Paleontological Museum, Mongolian Academy of Sciences, Ulan Baatar, Mongolia

CRETACEOUS (145–65 mya)

CENTROSAURUS

Centrosaurus was one of the most abundant of the large browsing ceratopsians at the end of the Cretaceous. Because fossils have been found concentrated in a thick layer, scientists believe that tens of thousands of these animals, roaming in large herds, were killed in a flood.

Centrosaurus's powerful front limbs would have enhanced this animal's speed and agility.

Discovery *Centrosaurus* was first described in 1876 by Edward Drinker Cope and incorrectly named *Monoclonius*, "single horn." It was renamed *Centrosaurus apertus* in 1904 by Lawrence Lambe. The layer of bones, which is widespread throughout the rich dinosaur deposits of Alberta, Canada, is now known as the *Centrosaurus* bone bed.

Characteristics This dinosaur had a well-developed frill that was made lighter by large holes (known as "fenestrae"). In life the frill and holes would have been covered with skin. Small tongues of bone hung downward from the top of the frill, and there was a large curved horn near the front of the snout. A number of species of *Centrosaurus* have been named, but they are now recognized as variations (possibly male–female differences) within a single species. As well as skeletons, some skin impressions of this dinosaur have been found.

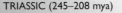

TRIASSIC (245–208 mya)   JURASSIC (208–145 mya)

KEY FACTS

Group Marginocephalia
Family Ceratopsidae
Genus *Centrosaurus*
 SENT-roh-SAW-rus
Meaning Sharp-point lizard
Size 20 feet (6 m)
Diet Plant-eater
Hip type Ornithischian
Region Alberta, Canada
Museums Royal Tyrrell Museum,
Alberta, Canada; American Museum of
Natural History, New York, USA

DEADLY WEAPONS
Centrosaurus could turn its
head swiftly and defend itself
against large predators such as
Tyrannosaurus with its short,
heavy head shield and sharp spike.

TRICERATOPS

Triceratops is one of the best known of all the dinosaurs and was the largest of the ceratopsian group. Over the years, some 16 different species have been named, but recent research has reduced this number to just two.

CHANGING IDEAS
Paleontologists used to think that *Triceratops* walked with its front legs bent (left). They now think that the front legs, like the hind ones, probably remained straight (right).

Discovery John Bell Hatcher found the first complete *Triceratops* skull in Wyoming in 1899. Over the next three years he collected another 30 skulls, most of them of *Triceratops*. Barnum Brown, too, collected many *Triceratops* skulls between 10 and 20 years later.

Characteristics *Triceratops's* massive head bore a short frill of solid bone along with the three large horns for which it is named—one above each eye and a smaller one on the snout. Traces of blood vessels found in the frill and horn have suggested to some scientists that the frill may have served as a means of regulating the animal's body temperature. As with other ceratopsians, the frill would probably have been covered with skin and may also have been used during courtship displays.

TRIASSIC (245–208 mya)   JURASSIC (208–145 mya)

SPIKY SHIELD

The back of *Triceratops*'s neck was a massive frill of solid bone with horns up to 3 feet (1 m) long that protected the vulnerable underside of the neck and chest from attack.

KEY FACTS

Group Marginocephalia
Family Ceratopsidae
Genus *Triceratops*
   try-SAIR-uh-TOPS
Meaning Three-horned head
Size 30 feet (9 m)
Diet Plant-eater
Hip type Ornithischian
Region Alberta, Saskatchewan, Canada; Colorado, Montana, South Dakota, Wyoming, USA
Museums American Museum of Natural History, New York, USA; Smithsonian Institution, Washington DC, USA; National Museum of Natural Sciences, Ottawa, Canada; National Museum of Natural History, Paris, France; Natural History Museum, London, UK; Royal Scottish Museum, Edinburgh, UK; Senckenberg Nature Museum, Frankfurt, Germany

CRETACEOUS (145–65 mya)

Everyday living *Triceratops's* habits were probably quite similar to those of the lumbering modern herbivore, the rhinoceros. Its many rows of closely packed grinding teeth suggest that it fed on a range of coarse vegetation, such as ferns, conifers and cycads, as well as on some of the flowering plants that appeared in the late Cretaceous. It cropped this plant matter with its long, powerful, pointed horny beak. Its jaw mechanism was adapted for cutting. Large jaw muscles attached from the lower jaw up onto the frill and powered the shearing action of the jaws.

There till the end *Triceratops* was one of the last known dinosaurs. Isolated horn cores

LOCKING HORNS
Two huge *Triceratops* prepare to do battle in the quest for a mate.

WELL PROTECTED
This skeleton of *Triceratops horridus* shows its formidable armory of three horns and a bony neck plate.

belonging to this dinosaur show that, along with its main predator, *Tyrannosaurus*, *Triceratops* persisted right to the end of the Cretaceous. The abundance of *Triceratops* fossils from the latest part of that period provides convincing evidence of this dinosaur's ability to survive, despite the numerous predatory theropods that shared its territory.

CHASMOSAURUS

One of the earliest of the longer frilled dinosaurs, *Chasmosaurus* was a moderate-sized neoceratopsian. This dinosaur is now known from several skulls and skeletons.

Chasmosaurus's *frill had right-angled upper corners with small ornamental horns.*

TRIASSIC (245–208 mya)   JURASSIC (208–145 mya)

BATTLE FOR DOMINANCE

Two *Chasmosaurus* stags engage in a courtship battle. The huge frill was covered with skin which may have changed color when the male animals indulged in courtship displays.

KEY FACTS

Group Marginocephalia

Family Ceratopsidae

Genus *Chasmosaurus*
KAZ-moh-SAW-rus

Meaning Chasm lizard

Size 17 feet (5 m)

Diet Plant-eater

Hip type Ornithischian

Region Texas, USA; Alberta, Canada

Museums Royal Ontario Museum, Toronto, Canada; Australian Museum, Sydney, Australia

Discovery Lawrence Lambe discovered *Chasmosaurus* on the Red Deer River in Alberta, Canada. He named it in 1914 for the chasm in which he found it.

Characteristics *Chasmosaurus* had a small horn on its snout and two slightly larger, upwardly curving horns above its eyes. At the back of its long, narrow skull was a huge bony frill that stretched over the animal's back and shoulders. Within the frill were two enormous openings, or fenestrae, which made the frill much lighter than that of any of its relatives. The bony part of the frill consisted of little more than a framework for the openings. Early studies made on skulls from Alberta and the northern United States suggested that they belonged to several different species. Today, however, most paleontologists consider that the variations reflect male–female differences within one species—*Chasmosaurus canadensis*. Another species, *C. mariscalensis*, from Texas, is known from pieces of the skull and isolated bones which together make up an almost complete skeleton. *C. mariscalensis* had larger, more backward-curving horns than *C. canadensis*.

CRETACEOUS (145–65 mya)

TOROSAURUS

Torosaurus was one of the most advanced of the long-shielded neoceratopsians. In terms of length, *Torosaurus* was not much smaller than its close relative *Triceratops*, but because of its slender build, it probably weighed considerably less.

Discovery John Bell Hatcher discovered a skull of *Torosaurus* in Wyoming in 1889. He sent it to Othniel Charles Marsh, who named it in 1891, in recognition of the bull-like size of its skull and its large eye horns. Partial remains of another four *Torosaurus* have been found and have resulted in the naming of several species. However, differences between them have been attributed to male–female variations.

A gigantic head *Torosaurus* had a gigantic head that measured more than 8 feet (2.5 m) long. Its skull was longer than that of any other land animal that has ever lived. Its neck frill, too, was enormous and made up about half the total skull length. The frill had two large, symmetrical openings that reduced its weight. *Torosaurus* was a plant-eater that sheared off tough plant matter with a sharp beak powered by its strong shearing jaws. It then ground this food with the many rows of teeth in the back of its mouth.

COMPARING SIZES
A human skull looks minuscule when set beside the vast skull and bony frill of a neoceratopsian such as *Torosaurus*.

TRIASSIC (245–208 mya)   JURASSIC (208–145 mya)

KEY FACTS

Group Marginocephalia
Family Ceratopsidae
Genus *Torosaurus*
    TAW-roh-SAW-rus
Meaning Bull lizard
Size 25 feet (7.5 m)
Diet Plant-eater
Hip type Ornithischian
Region Wyoming, South Dakota, Colorado, Utah, USA; Saskatchewan, Canada
Museums Peabody Museum of Natural History, New Haven, USA; Academy of Natural Sciences, Philadelphia, USA

Torosaurus had two prominent horns above the eyes and a very small horn on its snout. All three horns pointed forward.

CRETACEOUS (145–65 mya)

CLASSIFICATION TABLE

There are two basic groups of dinosaurs—the ornithischians and the saurischians—which are distinguished by having different hip structures. Beyond that, the classifications vary in rank and become quite complicated. The table below represents a simplification of the current state of knowledge of dinosaur classification.

ORNITHISCHIA GROUP

THYREOPHORA

	Family	Genus
	Scutellosauridae	*Scutellosaurus*
STEGOSAURIA	Stegosauridae	*Kentrosaurus*
		Stegosaurus
		Tuojiangosaurus
ANKYLOSAURIA	*Uncertain*	*Minmi*
	Nodosauridae	*Edmontonia*
	Ankylosauridae	*Ankylosaurus*

ORNITHOPODA

	Family	Genus
	Heterodontosauridae	*Heterodontosaurus*
	Hypsilophodontidae	*Atlascopcosaurus*
		Hypsilophodon
		Qantassaurus
		Tenontosaurus
EUORNITHOPODA	*Uncertain*	*Muttaburrasaurus*
	Iguanodontidae	*Iguanodon*
	Hadrosauridae	*Corythosaurus*
		Edmontosaurus
		Lambeosaurus
		Maiasaura
		Parasaurolophus
		Saurolophus

MARGINOCEPHALIA

	Family	Genus
	Pachycephalosauridae	*Stygimoloch*
CERATOPSIA	Protoceratopsidae	*Protoceratops*
	Ceratopsidae	*Centrosaurus*
		Chasmosaurus
		Torosaurus
		Triceratops

SAURISCHIA GROUP

SAUROPODOMORPHA

	Family	Genus
SAUROPODA	Brachiosauridae	*Brachiosaurus*
	Camarasauridae	*Camarasaurus*
	Diplodocidae	*Apatosaurus*
		Barosaurus
		Diplodocus
		Mamenchisaurus
	Titanosauridae	*Saltasaurus*
PROSAUROPODA	Anchisauridae	*Anchisaurus*
	Melanorosauridae	*Riojasaurus*
	Plateosauridae	*Massospondylus*
		Plateosaurus

SEGNOSAURIA

Family	Genus
Therizinosauridae	*Segnosaurus*

THEROPODA

Family	Genus
Uncertain	*Eoraptor*
Herrerasauridae	*Herrerasaurus*
Coelophysidae	*Coelophysis*
Podokesauridae	*Dilophosaurus*

	Abelisauridae	*Carnotaurus*
	Ceratosauridae	*Ceratosaurus*
TETANURAE	Spinosauridae	*Baryonyx*
		Spinosaurus
		Suchomimus
	Megalosauridae	*Megalosaurus*
	Uncertain	*Cryolophosaurus*
	Allosauridae	*Allosaurus*
	Carcharodontosauridae	
		Carcharodontosaurus
		Giganotosaurus
	Coeluridae	*Ornitholestes*
	Tyrannosauridae	*Tyrannosaurus*
		Albertosaurus
	Compsognathidae	*Compsognathus*
	Coelurosauridae	*Sinosauropteryx*
	Troödontidae	*Troödon*
	Ornithomimidae	*Gallimimus*
		Struthiomimus
	Oviraptoridae	*Oviraptor*
	Alvarezsauridae	*Mononykus*
	Dromaeosauridae	*Deinonychus*
		Dromaeosaurus
		Velociraptor
	Aves	*Archaeopteryx*

GLOSSARY

ankylosaurs Members of a group of armored plant-eating dinosaurs that lived in North America, Asia, Europe and Australia by the late Cretaceous. They had thick skulls and barrel-shaped bodies that were protected by thick plates of bone and rows of spikes. They had a solid bone club at the end of their tails.

archosaurs A group of reptiles with certain shared skeletal features that includes the living crocodilians as well as the extinct dinosaurs and pterosaurs.

carnosaurs Large, heavily built theropod dinosaurs that included *Megalosaurus* and *Allosaurus*. Because of their size, they were relatively slow movers, and they probably scavenged carcasses as well as actively hunting living prey.

Cenozoic era The era that followed the Mesozoic, and began with the extinction of the dinosaurs 65 million years ago.

ceratopsians Late Cretaceous horned dinosaurs that flourished for about 20 million years. They included *Protoceratops* and *Triceratops* and were the last group of ornithischian dinosaurs to evolve before the extinction of the nonavian dinosaurs at the end of the Cretaceous. They established themselves all over western North America and central Asia, where they lived in large herds.

ceratosaurs Medium-sized theropods distinguished by the small crests or bony horns on their snouts. Trackways made by *Ceratosaurus*, a late Jurassic predator from North America,

indicate that these predators probably hunted in packs to bring down larger dinosaurs.

coelurosaurs A group of small, light, delicately built, meat-eating saurischians that included *Struthiomimus*, *Coelurus*, *Gallimimus* and *Compsognathus*. Coelurosaurs (the name means "hollow-tailed lizards") lived from the late Triassic to the late Cretaceous period in North America, Europe and Africa.

coprolite A dinosaur dropping that has fossilized.

Cretaceous period The geological period that lasted from 145 to 65 million years ago. This period saw both the flowering and the extinction of the dinosaurs.

crocodilians The only surviving representatives from the archosaur group of reptiles. They include crocodiles, gharials, alligators and caimans.

cycad A primitive, palmlike tree that flourished in the Triassic and Jurassic periods.

gastroliths Stomach stones. Sauropods swallowed these stones to help them digest food.

Gondwana The southern supercontinent formed when Pangea split into two near the end of the Triassic. This process began to occur about 208 million years ago.

hadrosaurs A group of duck-billed dinosaurs that included *Hadrosaurus* and *Maiasaura*. Hadrosaurs were the most common and varied plant-eating ornithopods. They evolved in central Asia during the early Cretaceous and spread to Europe and North and South America.

ichthyosaurs Short-necked, dolphin-shaped marine reptiles that lived at the same time as dinosaurs. Ichthyosaurs gave birth to live young at sea—they did not come ashore to lay eggs.

Ichthyosaurus grew to 7 feet (2 m) long and is known from a variety of fossil types, including coprolites and stomach contents.

iguanodonts Large, plant-eating, ornithopod dinosaurs. Iguanodonts evolved in the mid-Jurassic and spread widely throughout the world: Their fossils have been found from the Arctic Circle to Australia. The group dominated the early Cretaceous period. *Iguanodon* is probably the best-known member of the group.

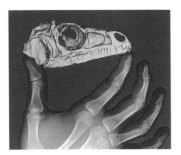

ilium The principal bone of the pelvis. The ilium, which is attached to the backbone, supports the legs.

ischium One of the bones of the pelvis. In dinosaurs, the ischium pointed downward and supported the muscles of the legs and tail.

Jurassic period The second geological period in the Mesozoic era. The Jurassic lasted from 208 to 145 million years ago.

Laurasia The northern supercontinent that formed when Pangea split into two toward the end of the Jurassic. It included present-day Europe, North America and most of Asia.

mammals A group of backboned animals that have hair and feed their young milk.

Mesozoic era The era, often called the age of reptiles, that spanned the Triassic, Jurassic and Cretaceous periods. It lasted from 245 to 65 million years ago. All of the nonavian dinosaurs lived during the Mesozoic.

meteorite A mass of rock or metal that has fallen to Earth from outer space. It comes from an asteroid.

ornithischians "Bird-hipped" dinosaurs. In this group the pubis pointed back and down, parallel to the ischium. All ornithischians were plant-eaters. This group included the ornithopods, stegosaurs, ankylosaurs and ceratopsians.

ornithopods "Bird-footed" ornithischian dinosaurs. This group included the pachycephalosaurs, iguanodonts, hadrosaurs and the horned, armored and plated dinosaurs.

pachycephalosaurs Plant-eating, bipedal, late Cretaceous ornithopod dinosaurs with skulls thickened into domes of bone. They included *Prenocephale* and *Pachycephalosaurus*. Pachycephalosaurs lived in Asia and North America.

Pangea The supercontinent that formed in the Permian period and broke up during the Jurassic.

plesiosaurs Large, fish-eating marine reptiles of the Mesozoic era. Plesiosaurs were generally long-necked.

pliosaurs Plesiosaurs with short necks and thick, powerful bodies.

prosauropods Late Triassic to early Jurassic ancestors of the long-necked sauropods.

pterosaurs Flying reptiles, only distantly related to dinosaurs. Pterosaurs evolved during the late Triassic period.

pubis A bone of the pelvis that pointed forward and downward in saurischians, but backward and parallel to the ischium in ornithischian dinosaurs.

saurischians "Lizard-hipped" dinosaurs. In this group the pubis pointed toward the head of the

pelvis. The saurischian dinosaurs are divided into two-legged, meat-eating theropods and four-legged, plant-eating sauropods.

sauropods Large, plant-eating, saurischian dinosaurs. Sauropods evolved during the late Triassic, and included the largest land animals ever to have lived.

species A group of animals or plants that can breed with each other and produce young that can also breed.

stegosaurs Late Jurassic dinosaurs that had alternating or staggered rows of plates along their backs, and two pairs of long, sharp spikes at the end of their strong tails.

theropods A group of saurischians that included all the meat-eating dinosaurs, from small predators such as *Coelurus* and *Compsognathus* to huge hunters such as *Tyrannosaurus* and *Spinosaurus*.

trackway A series of footprints that is left as an animal walks over soft ground.

Triassic period The first period of the Mesozoic era. It lasted from 245 to 208 million years ago.

vertebrae Bones, from the back of the skull to the tail, that protect the spinal cord.

INDEX

Page references in *italics* indicate illustrations and photos.

ACKNOWLEDGMENTS

TEXT Michael K. Brett-Surman, Christopher A. Brochu, Colin McHenry, John Long, John D. Scanlon, Paul Willis

ILLUSTRATIONS Anne Bowman; Simone End; Christer Eriksson; Cecilia Fitzsimons (Wildlife Art Agency); Chris Forsey; John Francis (Bernard Thornton Artists, UK); Lee Gibbons; Gino Hasler; Phil Hood (Wildlife Art Agency); Mark Iley (Wildlife Art Agency); Steve Kirk (Wildlife Art Agency); David Kirshner; Frank Knight; James McKinnon; Stuart McVicar; Colin Newman (Bernard Thornton Artists, UK); Nicola Oram; Marilyn Pride; Tony Pyrzakowski; Andrew Robinson (Garden Studio); Barbara Rodanska; Luis Rey (Wildlife Art Agency); Peter Schouten; Peter Scott (Wildlife Art Agency); Ray Sim

PHOTOGRAPHS American Museum of Natural History; Auscape; Australian Picture Library/Corbis; Bruce Coleman Collection; David Gillette; François Gohier Photography; Hammer & Hammer Paleotek; Humboldt Universität zu Berlin, Museum für Naturkunde; Institute of Vertebrate Paleontology and Paleoanthropology, China; Jura Museum, Germany; Musée National d'Histoire Naturelle; Museum Hauff; Museum of Natural Sciences; NASA; Natural History Museum, London; North Wind Picture Archives; O. Louis Mazzatenta; Patrick Cone Photography; Photodisc; Photolibrary.com/Science Photo Library; Planet Earth Pictures; Queensland Museum; Robert P. Stahmer; Royal Tyrrell Museum of Paleontology; Tom and Pat Rich; University of Chicago; Western Australian Museum; Weldon Owen; Zofia Kielan-Jaworowska